C000179355

mini Oman

The Essential **Visitors'** Guide

Oman mini Explorer
ISBN – 978-976-8182-89-0

Copyright © Explorer Group Ltd 2008
All rights reserved.

All maps © Explorer Group Ltd 2008

Front cover photograph: Musandam by Pamela Grist

Printed and bound by
Emirates Printing Press, Dubai, UAE

Explorer Publishing & Distribution
PO Box 34275, Dubai, United Arab Emirates
Phone (+971 4) 340 8805   Fax (+971 4) 340 8806
Email info@explorerpublishing.com
Web www.explorerpublishing.com

Introduction

The *Oman Mini Explorer* is a pocket-sized parcel of essential information that will help you make the most of your trip to this majestic country. It covers sights, culture, history, activities and the best places for eating and drinking. It is written by Oman residents, and brought to you by the same team responsible for the *Oman Explorer: The Complete Residents' Guide*. If you want to know more about what we do, or tell us what we've missed, go to www. explorerpublishing.com.

Editorial Team: Helen Spearman, Katie Drynan, Richard Greig and Grace Carnay
Contributing Author: Lucie Cruickshank
Designer: Hashim Moideen
Photographers: Pete Maloney, Pamela Grist, Jane Roberts, Mark Grist and Victor Romero

Contents

2 **Essentials**
4 The Gulf's Countryside
6 Oman Checklist
16 Best Of Oman
18 Getting Around
22 Local Knowledge
28 Public Holidays & Annual Events
32 Places To Stay

40 **Exploring**
42 'The Pearl Of Arabia'
46 At A Glance
48 Qurm & Shati Al Qurm
56 Muscat Old Town
62 Mutrah
68 Ruwi
74 Al Bustan, Sidab & Qantab
80 Madinat Sultan Qaboos & Al Khuwayr
86 As Seeb & Rusayl
92 Oman Areas
102 Tours & Safaris
110 Further Out

112 **Sports & Spas**
114 Sports & Activities
116 Watersports
120 Golf
124 Spas & Well-Being

128   **Shopping**
- **130**   Shop Oman
- **134**   Hotspots
- **138**   Shopping Malls
- **142**   Souks & Markets
- **146**   Where To Go For...

148   **Going Out**
- **150**   Omani Eats
- **152**   Venue Directory
- **154**   Qurm & Qurm Heights
- **158**   Shati Al Qurm
- **164**   Ruwi
- **166**   Al Bustan, Sidab & Qantab
- **170**   Madinat Sultan Qaboos
- **172**   Al Khuwayr
- **174**   Al Ghubbrah

176   **Profile**
- **178**   Culture
- **182**   History
- **186**   Oman Today

188   **Index**

Essentials

4 The Gulf's Countryside

6 Oman Checklist

16 Best Of Oman

18 Getting Around

22 Local Knowledge

28 Public Holidays & Annual Events

32 Places To Stay

The Gulf's Countryside

Stunning landscapes and magical waters make Oman one of the Gulf's best-kept secrets. For now.

Nestled in the south-eastern quarter of the Arabian Peninsula, with a land area of 300,000 square kilometres, the Sultanate of Oman is phenomenally diverse. Incredible geography comprising mountains and wadis, bustling city centres and serene beaches, pure waters and luxurious shores, means it has something for everyone.

The city centres are devoid of skyscrapers, giving Oman an old-world charm. Stout, pretty, white-washed buildings sit alongside ornate mosques and, in Muscat in particular, you'll see many places have a golden glow thanks to a gilt-inspired architectural style resplendent of an otherworldly wealth. Oman is a country that is proud of its ancestry and age-old traditions and you'll be pleased to discover an abundance of cultural attractions. Get out and about and explore numerous forts, ancient cities, museums and souks, or take in the excitement of the camel races.

Once off the beaten track, Oman's flora and fauna is equally appealing – more than 1,200 native plant species, including its native frankincense tree (Boswelia sacra) thrive in the Sultanate. Look out for the wonderfully wide variety of indigenous wildlife, including many endangered species such as the Arabian oryx, leopard and tahr (a mountain goat now only found in Oman). Its waters are home to more than 150 species of commercial shell and non-shell fish and 21 species of whales and dolphins, including the humpback whale. There are four species of sea turtle that come ashore to lay their eggs. You can see all of this firsthand.

Oman is unique perhaps in that every corner of the country has something special to offer. Adventure seekers will enjoy activities such as desert driving, wadi bashing, diving and trekking. Even if you're not keen to get active, the stunning natural beauty should be enough to keep you entertained. Though much of the country is barren desert, a brief shower quickly brings out the wild flowers. Coconut, banana and other tropical fruit trees thrive in the Salalah region in the south, whereas up north lagoons and fjords offer a completely different perspective.

Once you finally stop to catch your breath, you'll find the locals warm and welcoming, and restaurants serving up excellent fish, meat and vegetarian options, inspired by both local and international cuisine.

Over the next few pages you'll find vital information to help you plan your trip, plus advice on what to do when you first arrive. The things that you really shouldn't miss start on the next page. The Exploring chapter (p.42) divides Muscat into manageable chunks and showcases the best of the country's other areas. In Sports & Spas (p.118) you'll find out what Oman has to offer sports fans, and those who simply prefer to be pampered. Shopping (p.140) is your guide to malls, boutiques and souks. Going Out (p.172) reviews Muscat's restaurants, bars and clubs, while Profile (p.246) puts it all in context.

Oman Checklist

01 Spot Some Dolphins

It's practically the norm to see dolphins in the
glistening waters of the Gulf of Oman. However, the
chance of spotting a whale is much smaller, so keep
your eyes peeled; your patience might be rewarded.
See p.102.

02 Wait For The Turtles

Watching nesting turtles lumber up the beach to lay
their eggs, then make their way back into the sea, is
to see nature at its most miraculous. You are virtually
guaranteed a sighting in Ras Al Jinz Turtle Reserve
(p.105) where you can also camp overnight.

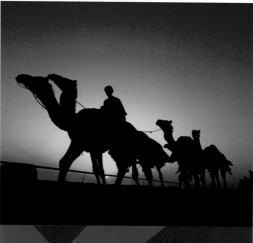

03 Ride A Camel

The experience of being atop an ungainly yet surprisingly graceful camel is one you won't forget in a hurry (p.106). If you'd prefer to keep your distance, get involved in the competitive camaraderie as a spectator at a camel race (p.114).

04 Tame The Wadis

Oman's wadis (dry gullies carved through rock by rushing water) are often filled with running water, and offer spectacular driving opportunities for off-road enthusiasts. Navigate narrow rocky tracks, or wallow in one of the freshwater pools. See p.104.

05 Explore Muscat's Past

The Natural History Museum in Muscat (p.48) offers a fascinating and informative tour of the wildlife of Oman. For an insight into the traditions and lifestyles of the locals, head to the Bait al Zubair Museum (p.56), which is located in a beautifully restored house.

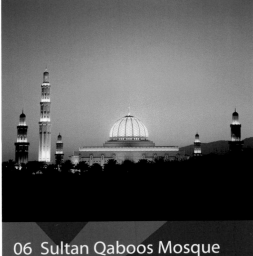

06 Sultan Qaboos Mosque

The external grandeur of the Sultan Qaboos Grand Mosque in Muscat is striking, and inside is no less spectacular. It is one of the largest in the Arab world and also one of the highest, with one of its minarets reaching almost 100 metres in height. See p.104.

07 Discover Nizwa

Nizwa was once the capital of Oman and the centre for trade between the coastal and interior regions. The town is embedded in a beautiful palm oasis, with a surprisingly large fort and a variety of souks, making it an absolute must visit. See p.96.

08 See Sinbad's Sohar

While you're in Oman you just can't miss out on
a trip to Sohar (see p.95), the birthplace of the
legendary Sinbad the Sailor. For a taste of the past,
the Sohar Fort Museum is the ideal place to learn all
about local history.

09 Admire Dhow Craft

Watch these traditional boats being built by hand in the dhow yard at Sur (p.100). The building process can take up to 12 months, but once finished the boats have a life of 100 years or more. If you've got the time, book a dhow cruise (p.102).

10 Get Lost In Mutrah Souk

Mutrah Corniche is a delight for any number of reasons, but a visit to Oman, never mind Muscat, wouldn't be complete without a stroll through its atmospheric souk (p.144). Discover for yourself why it's rated as one of the best in the region.

Best Of Oman

For Adrenaline Junkies...

Adrenaline junkies will find plenty to keep them occupied in Oman, whether it's underwater caves and wrecks for the experienced diver (p.116), hiring a 4WD and heading into the mountains, (p.99), mountain-biking or quad biking. See p.102 for a list of local Tour Operators throughout the country and check out Tours & Safaris in the Exploring section for an example of some of the organised options on offer. It doesn't have to be all heart-stopping action in the dunes or mountains; trying a new local or Arabic speciality when dining out can often be enough to awaken the senses (see p.152 for restaurants). However, if you're an out and out adventurer, you might want to pick up a copy of Explorer Publishing's *Oman Off-Road*, it's packed with exciting options for unforgettable weekends.

For Big Spenders...

If you've got the cash to splash then the first place you should be headed is Bustan and checking into the Al Bustan Hotel (p.34), one of the best in the world and a rare luxury treat. Once you've dined and explored your way around the city, hop on a domestic flight down south to Salalah (p.97) where you can spend your hard-earned cash on beautiful, traditional wares and artefacts. And if you really have more to spend, you can always buy a Persian rug and Omani antiques and get them shipped back home, which should put a nice dent in your wallet.

For Budget Travellers...

You don't have to spend a fortune to enjoy yourself in Oman. Although budget accommodation is best avoided, there are plenty of hotels and rest houses (p.32) that won't break the bank. Alternatively, if you're the outdoorsy type and have the gear, there are lots of scenic spots to set up camp. Try the Turtle Beach Resort in Ras Al Hadd (25 540 068) or the Arabian Oryx Sanctuary (www.oryxoman.com) in Jaaluni, six hours from Muscat by car. In the evening, there are many local kebab shops and cheaper restaurants (p.152) where you'll be served up a delicious feast for just a few baisas.

For Families...

Omanis are very family-oriented and you won't find it hard to entertain the whole gang here. Most hotels have special kids' entertainment sections, children's dining menus, and even offer babysitting services and playgroups. Al Sawadi Beach Resort (p.35) is particularly good, and is equipped with a kids' pool and a huge playground. The Oman Dive Centre (p.37) about 45 minutes' drive from Muscat airport is also an excellent choice. It has barasti huts providing unusual accommodation, a sheltered cove offering safe, supervised waters and a family-friendly restaurant. Oman boasts beautiful beaches and a stunning coastline, which all makes for a great family day out. Take a picnic to the beach, teach them to snorkel or take a boat and maybe spot some dolphins or exotic marine life along the way. See p.102.

Getting Around

Oman is easily navigated by car, taxi, bus or boat – just don't bank on walking too far in the summer months when temperatures soar.

Air

Oman Air operates direct flights to various regional destinations (24 707 222 for ticket sales, 24 519 223 for flight information, www.oman-air.com). Muscat International Airport (formerly Seeb International Airport) is located 35 kilometres from Muscat. It offers domestic flights to Salalah and Khasab (Musandam). Both Salalah and Muscat airports are undergoing significant expansion.

Airlines

Airline	Phone	Website
Air France	24 704 318	www.airfrance.com
British Airways	24 568 777	www.britishairways.com
Emirates Airline	24 792 222	www.emirates.com
Etihad Airways	24 823 555	www.etihadairways.com
Gulf Air	24 703 222	www.gulfairco.com
Kuwait Airways	24 701 262	www.kuwait-airways.com
Lufthansa	24 708 986	www.lufthansa.com
Oman Air	24 707 222	www.oman-air.com
Qatar Airways	24 787 070	www.qatarairways.com
Saudi Arabian Airlines	24 789 485	www.saudiairlines.com
Singapore Airlines	24 791 233	www.singaporeair.com

Boat

There are no scheduled passenger services from Muscat to other countries. Walk along the coast however, and you can easily hire fishing boats or dhows for daytrips. Those from Khasab are particularly recommended (p.99).

Bus

The Oman National Transport Company (ONTC) has a fleet of buses and coaches servicing the whole of Oman, and also the UAE. The buses cover all areas of Muscat, and timetables, destinations and route numbers can be found at the bus stops (marked with a red bus on a green sign) at the side of the road. Make sure you have the exact change ready. Long-distance routes depart from Ruwi in Muscat. You can find more information at www.ontcoman.com.

Car Rental

You'll find all the main rental companies, plus many local firms, in Muscat and Salalah. The larger, more reputable firms generally have more reliable vehicles and a greater capacity to help in an emergency. Make sure that you get comprehensive insurance and that it includes personal accident coverage. Most international and foreign licences are accepted but residents will need an Omani licence to rent a car. If you are using a rental car and you're caught speeding or commit some other driving offence, don't think you'll get away with it because you're a tourist. Tickets for speeding and parking offences can be charged to your credit card, sometimes weeks after your departure.

Driving

Driving is on the right-hand side of the road and seatbelts are mandatory in the front seats. The use of mobile phones while driving is banned. Driving is pretty rough and ready so keep your wits about you and be prepared for anything. In the event of an accident, contact the police on 999. There is strict zero tolerance of drink driving and penalties are severe. You should always keep your licence on you.

Taxi

Taxis are very common, are always driven by an Omani national, and all provide seatbelts. They are white with distinctive orange stripes, but not all are metered so be prepared to arrange the price before you get in – and don't

Car Rental Agencies	
Al Masky Rent-A-Car	24 595 241
Avis Rent-A-Car	24 607 235
Budget Rent-A-Car	24 794 721
Discovery Car Rental	24 833 646
Europcar	24 700 190
General Automotive Co LLC	24 492 143
Global Car Rental	24 697 140
Hertz Rent-A-Car	24 566 208
Sixt	24 482 793
Thrifty	24 489 248
Toyota Rent-A-Car	24 561 427
Value Plus Rent-A-Car	24 817 964

Alternative transport

be afraid to negotiate. Just flag one down and hop in. City Taxi (24 603 363) and Hello Taxi (24 607 011) are private taxi firms that you can call in advance to reserve but it's often a good idea to call nearer the time to confirm.

Walking

If you limit your exploring to specific 'pocket' areas, walking is an enjoyable way to see some of the natural beauty of the country, especially Muscat's old town, and the Mutrah area. In the cooler months the beaches and mountains of Oman can provide good exercise, with stunning views.

Local Knowledge

The most important thing is that you enjoy yourself, so make sure you're one step ahead of any glitches.

Banks & ATMs

Banking hours are usually 08:00 to 12:30, Saturday to Wednesday – some banks do open on Thursdays for a few hours between 08:00 and 11:30. Most ATM machines accept a wide range of cards, including Mastercard, Visa, American Express, Global Access, Plus System and Cirrus. ATMs can also be found in shopping malls, at the airport and at various street locations.

Climate

Sunny blue skies and warm temperatures are the norm year round. The best time to visit Oman is in winter, between October and April when temperatures average between 25°C and 35°C during the day and about 18°C at night. Summer temperatures in the north can reach 48°C during the day, and average 32°C at night. Humidity can rise to 90%. The southern Dhofar region receives light monsoon rains between June and September.

Crime & Safety

While street crimes are uncommon in Oman and violent crimes are rare, it is wise to maintain a healthy degree of caution. Ladies are strongly advised to avoid taking the orange and white taxis if they are alone as there have been cases of harassment. Men stare but you can minimise the hassle by dressing modestly and staying away from lower-end hotels. Staring tends to be worst on the public beaches, but generally if you can ignore it you'll save yourself a lot of aggravation. If that doesn't help, call the police on 999.

Disabled Visitors

Most of Oman's hotels have wheelchair access and toilet facilities for people with special requirements. There are also reserved parking spaces in most carparks. Some places do have wheelchair ramps, but often with incredibly steep angles. Always ask beforehand if somewhere has wheelchair access and make sure to get specific explanations – an escalator is considered wheelchair access by some.

Electricity & Water

The electricity supply is 220/240 volts. Sockets are the three-pin UK system. The tap water is safe to drink but can taste chlorinated. Local bottled water is a cheap alternative and there are many brands to choose from.

Health Requirements

No health certificates are required for visitors coming in to Oman, except for those who have recently been in a yellow fever-infected area. If this is the case, you will need a certified vaccination at least 10 days before arriving. Travellers from Africa may be spot-tested for malaria on arrival. Vaccination for Hepatitis A and B, and typhoid is recommended. Check the

World Health Organisation website (www.who.int/ith/en) or
try www.fco.gov.uk for more information.

Money

The monetary unit is the Omani rial (RO or OR) and is tied
to the US dollar at a mid-rate of approximately $1: RO.0.385.
The rial is divided into 1,000 baisas and notes come in
denominations of 50, 20, 1, ½ (500 baisas), ¼ (250 baisas),
200 baisas and 100 baisas. Coin denominations are 50, 25,10
and 5 baisas. Denominations are written in both Arabic and
English. Cash is the preferred method of payment in Oman
but many larger stores and restaurants will accept credit
cards. Cash and traveller's cheques can be exchanged in
licensed exchange offices, banks and international hotels.
To avoid additional exchange rate charges, take traveller's
cheques in US dollars.

Dos & Don'ts

Although Oman is a fairly liberal country, there are a few
things to watch out for. When taking your holiday snaps,
adhere to signs banning photography and always ask
permission when taking photos of local citizens. If the
answer is 'no', respect that and don't push it. It's illegal to
drink alcohol in public places and the penalties are harsh.
The same goes for drink driving and for drunk and disorderly
behaviour. Be warned that it is illegal to bring alcohol into
Oman by road.

If you don't want unwelcome attention, dress
conservatively. This is even more important in rural areas

where you'll be considered offensive if you show too much skin, so cover up shoulders and knees. Also, it's a good idea to pack an extra layer when going to eat indoors or to the cinema as the air conditioning is often set to polar degrees.

Newspapers & Magazines
You can get a wide selection of English and foreign language press in Oman in bookshops, petrol stations, supermarkets, hotel bookshops and grocery shops. However, prices are usually higher than you're used to and often newspapers are a few days late. *The Oman Daily Observer*, *Times of Oman* and *Oman Tribune* (200 baisas each) are the three daily English newspapers. *The Week* is a free tabloid that comes out on Wednesdays, found on branded stands throughout Muscat.

Post & Courier Services
Post offices are generally open from 07:30 until 14:00, Saturday to Wednesday, and most open for a few hours in the evening. For larger packages, try Aramex (24 563 668, www.aramex.com), or DHL (24 563 668, www.dhl.com).

Telephone & Internet
Oman Mobile and Nawras both offer a pre-paid mobile phone SIM card kit that is compatible with any handset. These range in price from RO 9 to RO 30. You can buy top-up cards in supermarkets, petrol stations and smaller shops, as well as prepaid phone cards for use on any landline phones or payphones. Internet cafes can be found in most shopping malls in the bigger cities, and some restaurants have Wi-Fi.

Time, Business & Social Hours

Local time is +4hrs UCT (Universal Coordinated Time, formerly GMT) with no summer saving time, so the clocks don't change. Some businesses still close for a long afternoon break, (known as a 'split shift') but most of the private sector work straight shifts from 09:00 to 17:00 or 18:00. Government offices are open from 07:30 to 14:30, Saturday to Wednesday.

Tipping

Many hotels and restaurants automatically include a service charge of at least 5% (check the bottom of your bill). However, this is unlikely to end up with your waiter so a tip of a few hundred baisas is greatly appreciated. The same applies for petrol pump attendants and taxi drivers, hotel porters, and generally anyone providing a service.

Visas & Customs

There are four types of visa that are relevant to visitors – single entry, multiple entry, express, and common visa facility with Dubai. This last one is for visitors who have a valid visit for Dubai, meaning they can travel to Oman freely. A single entry visa that is valid for one month costs RO.6 and a multiple entry visa, valid for one year for stays of up to three weeks each, costs RO.10. Visa application forms are available before passport control, or look out for the Travelex counter if flying into Muscat. Be sure to verify your visa expiration date before you leave the immigration counter; a hefty RO.10 penalty per day is enforced should you overstay your welcome. For further information, see www.rop.gov.om.

Clockwise from top left: Mutrah Souk, Mutrah Fort, Sultan Qaboos Mosque

Oman's rich culture and diverse population means there is plenty going on all year round.

Public Holidays

Public holidays in Oman regularly involve grand celebrations and can often last a few days. Some dates are fixed while others are decided in line with the lunar calendar.

Eid Al Fitr is a three-day holiday that celebrates the 'Feast of the Breaking of the Fast' at the end of the holy month of Ramadan. Eid Al Adha, meaning 'Feast of the Sacrifice', is a four-day holiday marking the end of the annual pilgrimage to Mecca. The ritual involves the slaughtering of many animals and the giving of alms and food to the poor. The holiday is celebrated 70 days after Eid Al Fitr. Lailat al Mi'raj celebrates the Prophet's ascension into heaven. Oman's National Day is on 18 November, as is His Majesty's Birthday. Celebrations

Public Holidays	
Birthday of HM Sultan Qaboos	18 Nov
Eid Al Adha (moon)	Dec 9 to12 2008
Eid Al Fitr (moon)	Oct 2 to 4 2008
Islamic New Year's Day (moon)	Dec 29 2008
Lailat Al Mi'raj (moon)	Jul 20 2008
National Day	Nov 18
Renaissance Day	Jul 23

continue with parades, fireworks, camel races and bullfights
throughout the country. Over the summer months,
Renaissance Day commemorates the accession of His Majesty
Sultan Qaboos to the throne.

Annual Events

Fahal Island Swim
Fahal Island   http://omantriathlon.com/events.html
Every year in May, brave competitors get up at 06:00 to swim
four kilometres from Al Fahal Island to the Ras Al Hamra
Recreation Centre beach. Anyone can participate; swimmers
just need to fill in the entry form, pay the fee of RO.5 and
organise boat support.

Camel Racing
Various Locations
This traditional sport is incredibly popular and an important
part of Omani culture. Races are spread over several days with
prizes of up to RO.250,000. Events are held in As Seeb, Salalah,
the Interior and Batinah regions and during public holidays
and National Day celebrations. Admission is usually free.

Horse Racing & Show Jumping
Seeb   24 490 424
The Oman Equestrian Federation organises the Annual Royal
Meeting, national show jumping competitions every winter,
and the Royal Equestrian Show every five years at the Enam
Equestrian Grounds in Seeb.

Khareef Festival

Salalah   www.khareefsal.com

This festival is held in Salalah each year, from 15 July to the end of August, to celebrate the monsoon season. There are music and dance performances from different regions of Oman, the exhibition and sale of Omani handicrafts, and sports events.

Muscat Festival

Muscat
800 77 2006
www.muscat-festival.com

This 22 day event held in January and February in Muscat showcases Oman's vibrant history and culture with traditional dances, camel races, concerts, sporting and educational events, and various activities for adults and children.

Wahibas Challenge

www.omanlandrover.com

Usually held in October, this motorsports event involves crossing the Wahiba Sands from east to west in a 4WD. It's quite a test of skill and endurance, with contenders crossing about 31 dune ridges over 60 kilometres.

Rally Oman

www.rallyoman.com

Oman's premier motorsport event is usually held over three days in early April. Family entertainment is also on offer including a freestyle motocross competition, music concert and parachutists. Entrance is free.

Muscat Festival

Places To Stay

From barasti beach huts to five-star finery, visitors to Oman are spoilt for accommodation.

Oman has no shortage of places to stay, from luxury hotels to hotel apartments, rest houses, officially approved campsites and even desert camps for tourists. However, the cheap and cheerful market is limited, so try some of the smaller hotels or rest houses for more competitive rates. Visitors can expect attractive promotions during the summer months when occupancy rates are lower. However, during peak times, such as the khareef in Salalah or festival time in Muscat, it can be difficult to find a room, and advance booking is a must.

Hotel Apartments

Beach Hotel Apartments	Shati Al Qurm	24 696 601
Dhofar Park Inn International	Salalah	23 292 272
Khuwair Hotel Apartments	Al Khuwayr	24 789 199
Manam Hotel Apartments	Al Wutayyah	24 571 555
Safeer Hotel Suites	Mutrah	24 691 200
Seeb International Hotel	As Seeb	24 543 800

Rest Houses

Al Noorah Gardens	Madinat As Sultan Qaboos	99 322 247
Al Qabil Rest House	Al Qabil	25 581 243
Ghaba Rest House	Ghaba	99 358 639

The Chedi Muscat

Hotels In Muscat

Al Bandar Hotel

www.shangri-la.com   24 776 666

As well as the 195 rooms (all with balcony or terrace), Al Bandar
also has eight food and beverage outlets. At the heart of the
Barr Al Jissah Resort, it has a souk area selling upmarket brands,
and art and crafts. A large swimming pool snakes around the
hotel, with sunbeds immersed in water so that you can relax in
cool comfort. There is also a jacuzzi and a kids' pool.

Al Bustan Palace InterContinental Hotel

www.al-bustan.intercontinental.com   24 799 666

This award-winning hotel, which has undergone significant
restoration, nestles in a coastal oasis of 200 acres, fronting
rugged mountains and with its own private beach. The
elegant Arabic theme of the lobby carries over to its 250
suites, all with private balconies. There are four international
restaurants, including one of the best Chinese restaurants in
Oman (p.168).

Al Husn Hotel

www.shangri-la.com   24 776 666

Resembling an Omani fort, Al Husn is an escape from the
ordinary. Each of the 180 bedrooms have a balcony or terrace,
and bathrooms are designed to ensure you can see the sea
from your bath (which your butler will run for you, should you
wish). Al Husn has a private gym, a beach, an infinity pool and
a library, as well as some excellent restaurants and bars.

Al Sawadi Beach Resort

www.alsawadibeach.com   26 795 545

Visitors have the option of staying in one of the chalet-style rooms, or bringing a tent and camping on the private beach with access to the resort's facilities. Facilities include a pool, gym, tennis, squash and mini-golf. Windsurfing, waterskiing, jetskiing and kayaking are all available. The dive centre offers PADI courses and organises regular trips.

Al Waha Hotel

www.shangri-la.com   24 776 666

This is the largest of the hotels within Shangri-La's Barr Al Jissah Resort, with 302 bedrooms. Designed for families, kids will love the Little Turtles club, where they can play in air-conditioned comfort or outdoors. The hotel has numerous swimming pools, including a rubber-cushioned toddlers' pool and a kids' pool in the shape of a mushroom. Babysitting services are available.

The Chedi Muscat

www.ghmhotels.com   24 524 400

This beautiful luxury hotel, regularly voted among the world's best, is designed for relaxation. Guests have the choice of 119 rooms or 32 private villas from which to contemplate Muscat's Hajar Mountains and azure waters. There are spa facilities, two infinity pools, poolside cabanas and a private beach. The eponymous The Restaurant (p.175) offers excellent contemporary Asian and Mediterranean cuisine.

Crowne Plaza Hotel Muscat

www.cpmuscat.com 25 429 223

Located on a cliff overlooking Al Qurm town and beach, this hotel has one of the best viewpoints in Muscat. The outdoor pool seems to spill onto the beachfront below, which can be accessed by steps from the hotel gardens. It has three international restaurants, including the excellent Iranian restaurant Shiraz (p.156). There is a popular health club within the hotel.

Golden Tulip Seeb

www.goldentulipseeb.com 24 510 300

This handy hotel is located just 1.5 kilometres from Muscat International Airport. Guests can enjoy private beach facilities (across the road) and a host of other leisure facilities within the hotel. There are 177 rooms, including six luxurious suites. Le Jarden restaurant serves international buffet cuisine 24 hours a day, and there is a bar with a live band.

Grand Hyatt Muscat

www.muscat.hyatt.com 24 641 234

Most of the Hyatt's 280 rooms have sea views. The Grand Hyatt has a delectable range of dining options: Tuscany for Italian fare; Mokha Café for casual all-day dining; Marjan Beachfront Restaurant & Bar for food and drinks with a view, and the lively Copacabana nightclub (Muscat's most happening nightspot, p.163). The hotel's decor is often described as 'Disneyland meets Arabia'.

InterContinental Muscat

www.interconti.com   24 680 000

The InterCon is popular for its outdoor facilities, international restaurants, and pubs with regular live bands and entertainment. Alfresco restaurant Tomato is a must-try, as is Trader Vic's with its legendary cocktails. Some of the 265 rooms have views of Qurm Beach.

Oman Dive Centre

www.diveoman.com.om   24 824 240

Nestled in a sheltered cove, this popular collection of barasti huts offers charming, if rustic, accommodation. Perfect for water babies, boat and diving trips can be arranged and the alfresco restaurant will keep your energy up.

Radisson SAS Hotel

www.radissonsas.com   24 487 777

Just 15 minutes from Muscat airport, this medium-sized hotel stands out in the Al Khuwayr business district. Some of its 142 rooms have mountain views. There is a good health club and a complimentary shuttle bus to Qurm Beach.

Sheraton Oman Hotel

www.starwoodhotels.com   24 772 772

Five kilometres from Sohar town centre, this hotel offers 41 luxury guest rooms, suites and chalets (all with private balconies), and a choice of dining options. Leisure facilities include a pool, gym, tennis court and crazy golf course.

Hotels In Musandam

Golden Tulip Resort Khasab

www.goldentulipkhasab.com   26 730 777

The Golden Tulip is situated in a small cove at the foot of imposing mountains. Visitors can choose from guest rooms and suites or independent chalets. Eating and drinking options include a coffee shop, pool terrace, restaurant, and Darts pub. There's a swimming pool, and the hotel organises diving and fishing trips and dhow cruises.

Hotels In Nizwa

Nizwa Hotel

www.nizwahotel.com   24 680 000

The Nizwa Hotel benefits from a picturesque setting, with landscaped gardens and the Hajar Mountains in the distance. There are 40 guest rooms, all with private access to the central swimming pool. The Birkat Al Mawz restaurant serves international cuisine and the hotel has two comfortable bars.

Hotels In Salalah

Crowne Plaza Resort Salalah

www.crowneplaza.com   23 235 333

Set in a private garden beside the sea, this hotel features 119 rooms and nine suites. There are three pools, kids' facilities, a health and fitness centre and a miniature golf course. The Dolphin Beach Restaurant offers alfresco dining.

Al Husn Hotel, Muscat

Hilton Salalah

www.salalah.hilton.com　　　　　　　23 211 234

This is the only five-star hotel in Dhofar. Its simple exterior hides a luxurious domed lobby and mirror-like marble floors. Its beachfront location, 12km from Salalah's centre, allows guests to get away from it all and enjoy the hotel's facilities, including three international restaurants and a health spa.

Hotels In Sur

Sur Plaza Hotel

www.omanhotels.com　　　　　　　26 841 111

Located a few kilometres from the centre of Sur, this is a perfect base from which to explore the area, including the turtle nesting sites at Ras Al Hadd and Ras Al Jinz. The hotel offers 108 well-appointed guest rooms, and has a swimming pool, health club and gym.

Exploring

42 'The Pearl Of Arabia'

46 At A Glance

48 Qurm & Shati Al Qurm

56 Muscat Old Town

62 Mutrah

68 Ruwi

74 Al Bustan, Sidab & Qantab

80 Madinat Sultan Qaboos & Al Khuwayr

86 As Seeb & Rusayl

92 Oman Areas

102 Tours & Safaris

110 Further Out

'The Pearl Of Arabia'

With its enchanting landscapes and welcoming people, Oman will always reward intrepid explorers.

The fabled land of Sinbad the sailor, Oman was on the must-stop list of every explorer worth his weight in frankincense for centuries. Marco Polo is believed to have visited the area 50 years before famous Moroccan explorer Ibn Battuta, who started his pilgrimage to Mecca in 1325.

Unlike some of their neighbours, Omanis passionately treasure their heritage, and rightly so; its rich history makes this beautiful land that much more magical. Take full advantage and be sure to stop and take in the abundant remains of ancient cities.

They don't call Muscat the 'pearl of Arabia' for nothing. A visit allows you to discover a friendly and modern city of juxtapositions. It's a place embedded in culture, with many museums, famous souks and other commercial centres, framed by diverse topography.

There is no one place which you can visit to get a 'feel' of Muscat, the capital city. The areas are divided by low craggy hills and each part has its own distinctive character. The only way to do it is to explore and take in all that it has to offer.

After Muscat it's time to take off to other, more rugged regions of the country. Travelling north will bring you to the cities of Barka, Nakhal and Sohar. If time allows, the Musandam peninsula to the north-west is highly

recommended, with its main towns of Khasab and Bukha, and with scenery totally different from the rest of Oman. It features beautiful fjords and lagoons and is becoming an increasingly popular tourist destination. Travelling inland leads you to Rusayl, Rustaq, Nizwa, Bahla, Jabrin and also to the mountains of Jebel al Akhdar, an experience not to be missed if you enjoy total tranquility. Going south via the interior route, you will pass the cities of Fanja, Sumail, Ibra, Al Mudayr, Al Mintrib, Sur and Ra's al Hadd.

On the coastal route Tiwi village is worth a stop, as is the ancient city of Qalhat, if only for the fact that this historical city, now in ruins, was of such particular interest to Marco Polo and Ibn Battuta.

The Southern province of Dhofar, with its capital Salalah, provides a welcome change in climate in the hot summer months. While the rest of Oman is paralysed by heat, the monsoon (khareef) blowing off the Indian Ocean ensures a high percentage of rainfall, resulting in cool weather and incredible greenery.

If you have a touch of the wild wanderer in you, there's many an adventure to be had, from desert driving, wadi bashing, turtle watching and mosque tours to discovering ancient forts and heritage sites. Just call up one of the tour operators listed later in this chapter (p.119) to make arrangements. If you can't find exactly what you're looking for, they'll happily tailor a trip to suit.

At the back of the book you'll find a pull-out map of Muscat and a detailed overview map of the country to aid your exploring.

Ancient housing settlements

'The Pearl Of Arabia'

At A Glance

Culture, sunshine and adventure is all yours in Oman – here's where to find it.

Heritage Sites

Bahla Fort	p.95
Bait Naa'man	p.94
Bukha Fort	p.100
Hisn Al Khandat	p.93
Jabrin Fort	p.96
Jalali Fort & Mirani Fort	p.58
Kersa Fort	p.95
Khasab Fort	p.99
Mutrah Fort	p.64
Nakhal Fort	p.94
Sineslah Fort	p.100
Walled City of Bahla	p.95

Museums & Art Galleries

Al Madina Art Gallery	p.82
Bait Al Zubair	p.56
Bait Muzna Gallery	p.56
Children's Museum	p.48
Currency Museum	p.68
Marine Museum	p.100
Muscat Gate Museum	p.58
National History Museum	p.80
National Museum	p.68

Omani French Museum   p.58
Omani Museum   p.82
Omani Society for Fine Arts   p.50
The Sultan's Armed Forces Museum   p.70

Beaches & Parks
Bandar Al Jissah   p.76
Beach Promenade   p.52
Kalbouh Park   p.62
Majan Beach   p.52
Masirah Island   p.100
Nasseem Park   p.88
Qurm Heights Park   p.52
Qurm Park & Nature Reserve   p.50
Riyam Park   p.64
Seeb Beach Park   p.88

Main Attractions
Al Thowarah Hot Springs   p.94
Al Ayn Tombs   p.95
Amouage Perfumery   p.86
Bat Tombs   p.92
Camel Souk   p.93
Foton World Fantasia   p.88
Lost City of Ubar   p.109
Marah Land   p.50
Ostrich Breeding Farm   p.94
Rustaq Hot Springs   p.95
Sinbad's Wonder Centre   p.52

Qurm & Shati Al Qurm

Excellent shopping, great restaurants and the best beaches – this is the perfect all-round destination, no matter what time of year.

The area known as Qurm (meaning 'mangrove' in English) lies in the centre of the greater Muscat area. It is divided into two districts – Qurm and Shati Al Qurm – each with quite different characteristics. Home to lavish living and a magnet for shopaholics looking for their very own prize possession, there are also some great parks and beaches, making it an attractive spot for everyone.

Children's Museum
24 605 368

Near Qurm National Park, Al Qurm

There is plenty of button pressing, handle turning, pedalling, balancing, jumping and running space for kids to exhaust themselves at this packed museum. Kids of all ages will enjoy this interactive science museum. Solidly built displays clearly explain holography, lasers, the human body, energy, computers and many other fascinations of daily life. Admission is free for children under 6, but costs 100 baisas for children aged 6 to 12, and 300 baisas for children aged 12 and over. Open from 08:00 to 13:30, Saturday to Wednesday and 09:00 to 13:00 on Thursdays (closed on Fridays). From October to March, the museum is also open on Monday afternoons from 16:00 to 18:00. Map 1 🔟

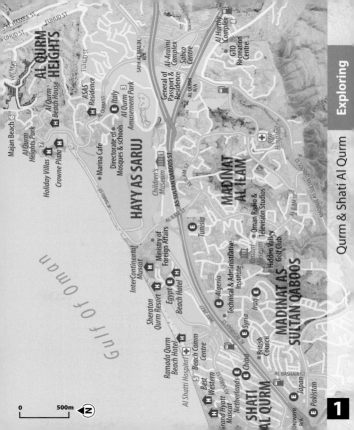

SHA HAMRA ST.

FUHUD ST.

FUHUD ST.

HRM ST.

AL QURM HEIGHTS

FUHUD ST.

Majan Beach 6

Al Qurm Heights Park

Al Qurm Beach House 7

Holiday Villas

Crowne Plaza

ASAS Residence

Al Qurm Amusement Park 3

Italy

General of Passport & Residence

SAYH AL MALIH R/A

Al-Araimi Complex

Sabco Centre

Al Harthy Complex

GTO Recreation Centre

AL QURM R/A

Directorate of Mosques & schools

Marina Cafe

Children's Museum

HAYY AS SARUJ

AS SAWMS ST.

AS SULTAN QABOOS ST.

AL ILAM ST.

MADINAT AL ILAM

Oman Radio & Television Studios

MADINA SAYH AL MALIH QABOOS ST.

RDP Hospital

Tunisia

Oman Museum

InterContinental Muscat

Ministry of Foreign Affairs

Egypt

Sheraton Qurm Resort

Beach Hotel

Algeria

Technical & Administrative Institute

Hidden Valley Golf Club

MADINAT AS SULTAN QABOOS

Iraq

Syria

AL ILAM ST.

Ramada Qurm Beach Hotel

Al Shatti Hospital

Beach Comm Centre

Best Western

China

British Council

Netherlands

AL SHATTI ST.

WAY WAY ST.

AL THARWAH ST.

Japan

SHATI AL QURM

Grand Hyatt Muscat

AL BASHAIR ST.

THUWAYR R/A

Pakistan

Gulf of Oman

0   500m   N

Marah Land (Land of Joy)
24 562 215

Qurm National Park, Al Qurm

Marah Land contains a boating lake and a fountain, as well as thrilling rides including the Space Gun, Flume Ride, Ferris wheel, bumper cars, the Giant Wheel, Horror Ride and rollercoaster. This place was designed with complete family entertainment in mind, and includes a variety of food outlets offering both Arabic and international munchies. Adults and children over 5 pay 300 baisas entrance fee, but children under 4 are free. You can buy a RO 1 package that includes 11 free games. Map 1 🙎

Omani Society for Fine Arts
24 694 969

Shati Al Qurm

Consider this a community where artists meet, share knowledge and display their work. The society holds regular exhibitions, meetings and events where people can learn more about a particular art form.

Qurm Park & Nature Reserve

Al Qurm St, Al Qurm

This sprawling park and nature reserve is Muscat's main park and features sprawling lawns, a boating lake, beautiful gardens and shady pergolas. It is the home of the Sultan's Rose garden and a large fountain, which is even more impressive at night when it's lit up. The Nature Reserve is made up of tidal wetlands and a mangrove nursery. The City Amphitheatre is also here, and can seat up to 4,500 people. Mondays are reserved for families only. Map 1 🗠

Muscat Festival

Sinbad's Wonder Centre
24 794 677

Al Harthy Complex, Al Qurm

There is a host of fairground rides to amuse big and little kids, with a section dedicated to computer and video games at this amusement park. You can bring your own food or get Sinbad's to cater in the separate dining area. Children will love the carousel, bumper cars and spinning teacups. Map 1 🔟

Beach Promenade

Near Grand Hyatt, Shati Al Qurm

In the early evenings, it seems that Muscat's entire population heads down to this beach to walk, jog, play football or just to have a paddle. You can enjoy it all without getting sand between your toes by stopping for a coffee or a bite at the nearby cafes and eateries. Map 1 🔟

Majan Beach

Near Ras Al Hamra Club, Qurm Heights

With its superb coral reefs Majan Beach is ideal for snorkellers. On good days you can see parrot fish, rays and turtles. The beach is equipped with man-made sunshades and barbecue pits. Map 1 🔟

Qurm Heights Park

Next to the Gulf Forum Hotel, Qurm

Shady trees and plenty of plants surround this park's grassy lawn, perched high on the cliffs over Qurm. At one end is a set of stone benches with Roman-style pillars where you can sit and forget about the rest of the world. Map 1 🔟

Clockwise from top: Qurm Park, Qurm Beach, Ras Al Hamra Beach

If you only do one thing in...

Qurm & Shati Al Qurm

Relax, unwind, take your shoes off and walk along the Beach Promenade (p.52).

Eating & Drinking: You can't come this far and not stuff yourself at Mumtaz Mahal (24 605 907).

Sightseeing: Get yourself to the Crowne Plaza (p.36). Perched on the edge of a clifftop, the views are breathtaking, as are the sundowners at The Edge.

Shopping: Home to one of Muscat's main shopping areas, there are three main malls to choose from: Al-Arami Complex, Capital Commercial Centre (CCC) (see p.130) and Sabco Commercial Centre (p.40).

Relaxation: Any of the many beaches and parks are perfect for some peace and quiet.

Families: Take your kids to the Qurm Park & Nature Reserve (p.50) for a great day out.

Sunset over Qurm

Muscat Old Town

Lap up the atmosphere at this coastal town, richly soaked in Omani culture and history.

This is a fantastic place to explore, particularly if you're after a glimpse of the past. You'll see many old houses that must have been here for generations, still being used by Omani families today, as well as the spectacular Al Alam Palace. This coastal town is relaxingly atmospheric, with much of the hustle based around its sheltered port.

Bait Al Zubair

Al Sadiyah St   24 736 688

A collection rather than a museum, the Bait Al Zubair offers a fascinating insight into the Omani traditions, mixing the ancient and the modern. Located in a beautifully restored house in Muscat, the four major displays cover men's jewellery, khanjars and male attire, women's jewellery and female attire, household items, and swords and firearms. There is also a fascinating photo gallery. Entry fee: RO 1 for adults and 250 baisas for children 10 to 15 years. Free for under 10s and school groups. Open from 09:30 to 13:00 and 16:00 to 19:00, Saturday to Thursday. Map 2 ▮

Bait Muzna Gallery

Opposite Bayt Al Zubair   24 739 204

This gallery first opened in 2000, yet is set in a traditional house that was originally built as a home for a member of

Tower

Gulf of Oman

MUSCAT

Mirani Fort

BAB AL MATHAIB ST

Council of the Ministries

Diwan of
Royal Court

Al Jalali
Fort

*Bait Muzna
Gallery*

ⓘ *Omani French
Museum*

Al Alam Palace

Royal Court
of Affairs

✚ *Diwan Clinic*

*Bait
Al Zubair*

• Ministry of Finance

AS SAIDIYA ST

0   200m   **N**

2

the royal family. It showcases the work of local talent and organises a number of workshops. The gallery sells fine arts and antiques, and offers a framing service. Map 2 **2**

Jalali Fort & Mirani Fort
Near Al Alam Palace

These two forts flank the Sultan's palace on the waterfront, overlooking Muscat Bay. Built on the site of earlier Omani fortifications, both forts were extensively renovated in the late 1500s by the Portuguese when they controlled Muscat. It takes some work to get entry into these due to their proximity to Al Alam Palace, but it's not impossible. You can get special permits to visit Jalali Fort by contacting the Ministry of National Heritage and Culture for more information (24 602555). Map 2 **3**

Muscat Gate Museum
Al Bahri Rd (inside city gates)   99 328 754

Located in one of the fortified gates of the old city walls, the Muscat Gate House is one of the newest museums to open its doors to visitors. It illustrates the history of Muscat and Oman from ancient times right up to the present day with a special display on the city's springs, wells, underground waterways, souks, mosques, harbours and forts. Map 2 **4**

Omani French Museum
Near Police Station, As Sadiyah Rd   24 736 613

On the site of the first French Embassy, this museum is a carefully preserved example of 19th century Omani

Muscat Gate Museum

architecture, celebrating the close ties between France and Oman over the past few centuries. The ground floor of the museum features exhibitions on early French contacts, the history of Omani-Franco trade and on HM Sultan Qaboos' visit to France. Upstairs you'll find records, furniture, clothes and photographs of early French diplomats. One room holds regional Omani women's clothing, and also some antique French costumes. Entry costs 500 baisas for adults and 200 baisas for children. Children under 6 enter free. The museum is open from 09:00 to 13:00, Saturdays to Thursdays. Map 2 🗺

If you only do one thing in...
Muscat Old Town

Immerse yourself in Oman's colourful history at Muscat Gate Museum (p.58).

Best for...

Eating & Drinking: Stop for some refreshment at one of the icecream vans along the Corniche, just what you need on those hot summer days.

Sightseeing: Don't knock, but do marvel at Sultan Qaboos' house, the striking Al Alam Palace.

Shopping: You can get the odd trinket from the museums, but it's not far to the shopaholic haven of Mutrah (p.62).

Relaxation: Wander through the recreation of a traditional mountain village at the Bait Al Zubair museum (p.56).

Families: Take your little ones on some cultural excursions through the many museums and forts in the area.

Al Alam Palace & Mirani Fort

Mutrah

Squeezed between the sea and a circle of hills, this tiny spot has grown into a vibrant port worth its weight in salt.

For a relatively small area, Mutrah packs a lot in. It is the perfect place to experience old world delights as you shop the old-fashioned way (in souks and with plenty of haggling), and watch Omani fishermen drag their catches into the harbour, as they have done for centuries. The souk (p.144) is an essential addition to any itinerary. You'll also find plenty of little street cafes to stop at and take in the sights, sounds and smells of this bustling port.

Hidden Treasures

If you're wandering through the souk in Mutrah, stop and take the time to rummage through the massive bowls overflowing with rings and bangles. Most of the souvenir shops have these and if luck is on your side, you may just find something really special.

Kalbouh Park

Situated along the coast by the village of Kalbouh, this small park is a picturesque spot for an evening stroll. As well as paved walkways, there's a stunning grassed amphitheatre that makes for perfect photo opportunities. A selection of kiosks and a small Pizza Hut sell snacks and drinks for when you need a quick pick me up. The scenery is

Gulf Of Oman

Port Sultan
Qaboos

MUTRAH

Corniche
AL MINA
R/A
Al Mina
FISH R/A
Al Nahda

RIYAM
R/A
Riyam
Park
2

Kalbuh
Park

AL BAHRI RD

Mutrah Souk

Sea View

Mutrah
1 Fort

Jibal Mutrah

Spain
E
Ar Rahma
Hospital

Ash Shijayiyah
Market

Trekking Path

MUTRAH ST

New Zealand

Muscat Dam

0   500m

N

3

spectacular, with the sea to one side and rocky hills to the other. During the day there is a beautiful view along the coast of Mutrah.

Mutrah Fort
Above Corniche

This is one of the few Portuguese forts left in the country. It was built about 1600 on a small outcrop of rock overlooking the corniche. In 1654 the fort was captured by the Omanis; a significant point in their fight to oust the Portuguese. There have been many additions over the years and it was fully restored in 1980 using traditional materials. Because it is still used by the authorities it is rarely open to visitors. However, you are allowed to take pictures of the building from the outside. Save your clicking for when it is lit up at night. Map 3 **1**

Riyam Park
Above Corniche

Riyam Park offers sublime views of the harbour. You can't miss it – it's the one with a gigantic white model of an incense burner perched on top of a hill. It is possible to walk up to the top of the structure. Admittedly it's a fairly steep climb but entirely worth it for the spectacular views. If the gate at the bottom is locked when you visit, you can still scramble up the side and over the wall to get access. The place is equally great for kids, with lots of playground equipment and even a small funfair. The funfair is usually open from 16:00, although check before you go to avoid disappointment as this varies from season to season. Map 3 **2**

If you only do one thing in...
Mutrah

Souk, souk and then souk some more – this is the place for a bargain hunt and rare finds.

Best for...

Eating & Drinking: Stop at one of the little cafes along the street for some local cuisine that won't break the bank.

Sightseeing: Mutrah Fort (p.64) is one of the few Portugese forts left in the country.

Shopping: Mutrah Souk (p.144) is famous and chock full of fabulous treasures.

Relaxation: It's got to be a 3km stroll along Mutrah Corniche on a warm evening.

Families: Climb the incense burner in Riyam Park (p.64), and really challenge the kids.

Mutrah Corniche

Ruwi

Brush up on some local culture, and enjoy fine dining and the bustle of a burgeoning district.

It has taken a mere 30 years to develop what was once a valley (Wadi Kabir) into the business epicentre of Muscat. Ruwi is also referred to as the central business district (CBD), and is now more notable for its modern architecture. Despite its business-centred atmosphere, the neighbourhood is full of kitsch souvenirs, and is the ideal place for a delicious Indian dinner.

Currency Museum

Central Bank of Oman, Opposite HSBC HQ   24 796 102

Located in the head office of the Central Bank of Oman, this museum showcases modern and historic coinage, as well as a gallery of Oman's currency throughout the years. However, it is not limited to Omani currency. You can also see various colonial currencies that were in circulation in the early 20th century, as well as coins and notes of regional importance. Entry costs 250 baisas. Open 08:00 to 15:00. Map 4 ▐

National Museum

Way 3123   24 701 289

A small but fairly comprehensive museum displaying silver jewellery, ladies' regional costumes, pottery, a selection of scale-built dhows, crockery, coffee pots and guns.

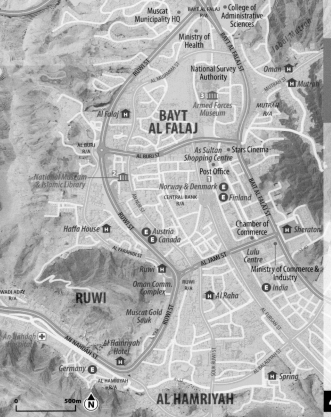

Muscat
Municipality HQ
BAYT AL FALAJ
R/A
College of
Administrative
Sciences

Ministry of
Health

RUWI ST

AL MUJAMMA ST

BAYT AL FALAJ ST

National Survey
Authority

Jabal M'utrah

Oman H

MUTRAH ST

H Mutrah

Al Falaj H

3 🏛
Armed Forces
Museum

BAYT
AL FALAJ

MUTRAH
R/A

AL BURJ
R/A

AL BURJ ST

As Sultan
Shopping Centre

Stars Cinema

BAIT AL FALAJ ST

National Museum
& Islamic Library

2 🏛

Post Office
1

Norway & Denmark E

AN NUR ST

CENTRAL BANK
R/A

E Finland

Haffa House H

RUWI ST

E Austria
E Canada

AL FARAHIDI ST

Chamber of
Commerce

H Sheraton

Lulu
Centre

Ruwi H

AL JAMI ST

Ministry of Commerce &
Industry

WADI ADAY
R/A

RUWI

Oman Comm.
Complex

RUWI
R/A

A Al Raha

E India

Muscat Gold
Souk

RUWI ST

AL FURGAN ST

An Nahdah
Hospital

AN NAHDAH ST

Al Hamriyah
Hotel

SOUK RUWI ST

AL BALADIYAH ST

H Spring

Germany E

AL HAMRIYAH
R/A

AL HAMRIYAH

0   500m

N

4

Additionally, there is a selection of unique items of furniture from the old palace in Muscat, clothes, pictures and medals from the Zanzibar rulers; as well as correspondence and pictures of the last five sultans in the Al Said Dynasty. Entrance costs 500 baisas for adults and 100 baisas for children (children under 6 are free). Open from 09:00 to 13:00 and 16:00 to 18:00 (October to March), and from 09:00 to 13:00 and 17:00 to 19:00 (April to September). Map 4 🄴

The Sultan's Armed Forces Museum

Bait Al Falaj Fort   24 312 654

This museum is set in the grounds of the Bait Al Falaj Fort, which was built initially as the garrison headquarters for Sultain Said bin Sultan's armed forces in 1845. You'll find features depicting the origins of Islam in Oman, tribal disputes and the many invasions of the coast by foreign powers. More recent military history is lavishly represented. Entry costs RO 1 for adults and 500 baisas for children. Open from 08:00 to 13:30, Saturday to Wednesday, and on Thursdays and Fridays from 08:00 to 11:00 and 15:00 to 18:00. Map 4 🄴

A Piece Of Silver

Maria Theresa (1717-1780), was wife and Empress of the Holy Roman Emperor Francis I. In 1751 the Maria Theresa thaler coin was introduced, at a time when Omani traders were desperately in need of an internationally acceptable and reliable currency. It was used until 1970 when Oman's own currency, the rial, was introduced.

Ruwi High Street

If you only do one thing in...

Ruwi

Take a stroll around the charming streets and soak up the atmosphere.

Best for...

Eating & Drinking: Dine at Golden Oryx restaurant (p.164) for great Thai and Chinese cuisine; this place has been feeding folk for the past 25 years.

Sightseeing: The Currency Museum (p.68), located in the head office of the Central Bank of Oman, is a fascinating diversion.

Shopping: The odd street vendor makes for an interesting stop along Ruwi High Street (p.135).

Relaxation: Dinner at the magnificent seafood buffet at the Sheraton (p.165), the tallest building in the area.

Families: Everyone will learn something at The National Museum (p.68).

Golden Oryx

Al Bustan, Sidab & Qantab

Al Bustan, Sidab & Qantab

Looking for something a little bit different? Stumble this way and you've found the perfect diversion from Muscat's other areas.

Even getting to this area is stunning. The spectacular mountain road from Ruwi takes you over the rise from Wadi Al Kabir, where you can see the village of Al Bustan nestled at the base of the hills with the sea in the background.

The Sohar dhow is a remarkable landmark and pays homage to the centuries of voyagers, on which the country's history is based, as well as its heritage and culture. Just past this is the Al Bustan Palace Hotel, one of the most famous hotels in the Gulf. You can spend a leisurely day drifting around the hotel grounds, have a cocktail on the beach or afternoon tea in the atrium. The whole thing is decadently beautiful and the service is five star.

The Seblat Al Bustan restaurant (p.169) offers a traditional Omani experience in Arabic tents set up in the hotel's gardens every Wednesday night throughout the cooler months. Even if your budget doesn't stretch to a night's stay in this luxury hotel, you should still experience the royal treatment with the legendary high tea in the Atrium Tea Lounge.

From the Al Bustan Roundabout you can head up the coast towards the scenic harbour area of Sidab. Fishing is the lifeblood of this area and traditions have been passed down through the generations. The Marine Science and Fisheries

Gulf of Oman

Barr Al Jissah

Yiti Beach

Al Waha H

Al Ahsan

Al Bandar

Shangri-La
Bar Al Jissah
Resort

Bandar Al Jissah

AL JISSAH

Qantab
Park

Oman Dive
Centre

QANTAB

AL JISSAH ST

HARAMIL

Haramil Village

Capital Area
Yacht Centre

Marina Bander
Al-Rowdha

Marine Fisheries
& Science Centre

SIDAB

Sidab
Sports Club

SIDAB ST

Jabal Ras al Burj

R.O.P
Directorate of Civil Defence
& Fire Prevention

QANTAB RD

Al Bustan
Palace H

AL BUSTAN

AL BUSTAN R/A

AL BUSTAN ST

To Yiti Beach

0   1km   N

Centre is an academic institution that undertakes studies of different fish stocks, but it also has a very interesting public aquarium and library where you can learn more about the area's aquaculture.

Further down the coast from Al Bustan, the mountains increase in height and the landscape gets more rugged. This undulating rocky coastline hides a number of beautiful secluded coves just waiting to be discovered.

Many of the bays in this area have stretches of sandy beach sheltered by the rugged cliffs, and crystal clear waters that are perfect for snorkelling, diving and fishing. At Qantab Beach you'll find a number of friendly local fishermen offering to take you out fishing (for a price, of course).

A little further south is the Oman Dive Centre (p.37), regarded as one of the top dive centres in the region.

Bandar Al Jissah

While this beautiful stretch of beach can be very busy on Fridays, its attractions are twofold – firstly it is accessible by 2WD car, and secondly it is the best place to catch a sea taxi. Sea taxis are the small fishing boats you see loaded up with fresh seafood during the week. On weekends, for a very small fee, they will transport you and all your gear to one of the secluded beaches such as Khayran, and leave you there until a specified time when they pick you up. It is widely understood that you need not pay the fee until you have been picked up. Don't forget to bring along your snorkelling gear as the marine life here is stunning.

If you only do one thing in...
Al Bustan, Sidab & Qantab

Dive. The aquatic life provides a brilliant escape from the hustle and bustle of the city.

Best for...

Eating & Drinking: The Seblat Al Bustan (p.169) offers the traditional Omani experience, complete with Arabic tents.

Sightseeing: If you can't afford to stay at the Al Bustan Palace Hotel (p.34), you should at least take in the incredible grounds.

Shopping: The Oman Dive Centre (p.37) has everything you'll need for underwater exploring.

Relaxation: A drive down Al Bustan Street out of Ruwi with the spectacular mountain backdrop will be enough to make you forget about the rest of the world.

Families: A beach taxi from Bandar Al Jissah beach (p.76) takes you to the clear waters off Khayran.

Shangri-La

Madinat Sultan Qaboos & Al Khuwayr

The treats to be found in Muscat's cosmopolitan home and shopping hub are well worth the trek.

On the other side of the main Sultan Qaboos highway is the leafy suburb of Madinat As Sultan Qaboos, lovingly referred to as MSQ. A few of the embassies are here as well as the British Council. There is a small but friendly shopping centre in the area.

Al Khuwayr is found towards central Muscat from Seeb, on the south side of the main road. It is home to a few ministry buildings, as well as some banks and embassies. The architecture is hugely impressive. Don't miss the Oman International Bank, the front doors of which are 10 metres high and plated in 24 carat gold, with an equally awe-inspiring interior. If you pass by early enough, you'll see the doors being polished every day. The Zawawi Mosque is also in this area, just off the main road.

Natural History Museum
Al Wazarat St   24 641 510

This museum, housed within the Ministry of National Heritage and Culture, has a fascinating and informative collection of exhibits relating to Oman's wildlife. If you're into stuffed animals (taxidermy, not toys). You can see animals in their different natural habitats, many of which are unique to Oman and the Gulf region, such as the Oryx and the

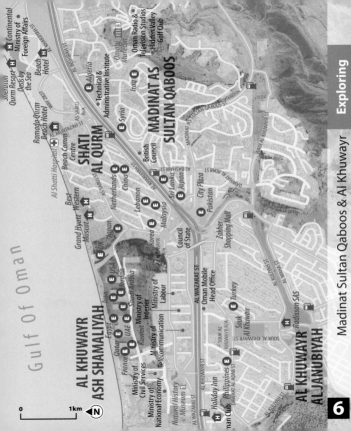

Gulf of Oman

AL KHUWAYR ASH SHAMALIYAH

SHATI AL QURM

MADINAT AS SULTAN QABOOS

AL KHUWAYR AL JANUBIYAH

Continental Qurm Resort
Ministry of Foreign Affairs
Oasis by the Sea
Beach Hotel
Ramada-Qurm Beach Hotel
Al Shatti Hospital

Oman Radio & Television Studios
Hidden Valley Golf Club
Oman Museum

Algeria
Technical & Administrative Institute
Iraq
Syria

Beach Comm Centre
Grand Hyatt Muscat
Best Western

British Council

Netherlands
China
Lebanon
Sri Lanka
Malaysia
Japan
Pakistan

City Plaza

Council of State

Zakher Shopping Mall

UK
Japan
Korea
USA
Jordan
Italy
Saudi Arabia
Ministry of Interior
Ministry of Labour

Egypt
UAE
Kuwait
Qatar
France

Ministry of Civil Services
Ministry of Telecommunication
Ministry of National Economy
National History Museum

Oman Mobile Head Office

Turkey
Souk Al Khuwayr
Radisson SAS

Holiday Inn
Oman Club
Philippines

Madinat Sultan Qaboos & Al Khuwayr

0   1km   N

6

Arabian leopard. The 'Oman Through Time' exhibition follows the history of the country through fossils, and includes the development of oil and gas reserves. Entry costs 500 baisas for adults and children aged 12 to 15 pay 300 baisas. Younger children get in for free. Map 6 🚺

Al Madina Art Gallery
Villa 1691, Road 2, MSQ   24 691 380

A one-stop-shop for many different forms of art in Oman, there are regular exhibitions of watercolours and oil paintings, as well as special events throughout the year. If you have some time to kill, browse through the large selection of prints. Al Madina also stocks interesting jewellery made from unconventional materials such as freshwater pearls and desert diamonds. If something like a genuine Omani wooden chest is on your shopping list, this is the place to buy an original instead of a foreign knock-off.

Omani Museum
Al Alam St, Way 1566, Near Ministry of Information 24 600 946

The Omani Museum sits atop Information Hill and is almost worth visiting for the view alone. It is run by the Ministry of Information, and though fairly small, is still very informative. It is the only museum in the capital that offers detailed archaeological information and artefacts. It also has displays on agriculture, minerals, trade routes, architecture, dhows, arts and crafts, jewellery and weaponry. Entry is free.
Map 6 🚯

Classical Omani doors and locks

If you only do one thing in...
Madinat Sultan Qaboos & Al Khuwayr

Buy some quality souvenirs from Al Madina Art Gallery (p.82).

Best for...

Eating & Drinking: Head to Pavo Real (24 602 603) for great Mexican in the heart of the Gulf.

Sightseeing: The Omani Museum (p.82) for its celebration of the country's culture.

Shopping: Al Fair (p.138) has everything you need and the odd thing that you can't live without.

Relaxation: Al Madina Art Gallery (p.82) is great for a slow mooch on a quiet afternoon.

Families: Check out the impressive opulence of Oman International Bank (p.80).

Sultan Qaboos Mosque

As Seeb & Rusayl

This may be on Muscat's outskirts, but what kind of adventure would it be if you didn't go beyond the city limits?

You might think that Seeb is a bit too far out of Muscat, but from Qurm it should take you less than 30 minutes to get here. Attractions include many parks and amusement centres, so it makes for a great daytrip, especially if you've got kids in tow. The Oman International Exhibition Centre (www.omanexhibitions.com) also hosts many interesting trade and consumer events in Seeb throughout the year. Rusayl, on the other hand, is home to one of the world's most renowned perfume factories.

You may already be familiar with the area after arriving at Muscat International Airport (formerly Seeb International Airport), where extensive refurbishment and the construction of a new passenger terminal are underway.

Amouage Perfumery
Rusayl   24 540 757

The factory produces the 'most valuable perfumes in the world', and the guided tour explains the production process as well as allowing visitors to test the fragrances. If you purchase a product you will receive a special gift. Traditional Omani coffee and dates are served during the visit. See www.amouage.com for more information. Entry is free. Open from 08:00 to 17:15, Sunday to Thursday. Map 7 **1**

Sohar

AL HAYL
ASH SHAMALIYAH

AL HAYT ASH SHAMALIYAH ST

Children's
Park

AS SUWAIQ ST / AS SEEB ST

AL AWBAK'S ST

As Seeb Beach
Park 5

Dream Oasis

AL MAWALIH
ASH SHAMALIYAH

AL HAYL
AL JANUBIYAH

ST 8

2 Markaz Al Bahja

MAZUN ST

AS SEEB ST

ST. 19

AL MAWALIH
AL JANUBIYAH

Muscat 3
City Centre

Muscat
International
Airport

ST. 17

Al Hayl
Souk

Amouage (Oman
Perfume Factory)
1

NIZWA RD

BURJ AS SAHWAH
R/A

Veterinary
Quarantine
Station

To Nizwa/Salalah

Naseem
Park

Al Rusayl
Centre

AS SULTAN QABOOS ST

Muscat

MUASKAR AL MURTAFAAH ST

AL MURTAFAAH ST

AL MURTAFAAH

To Ar Rusayl

0   3km   N

7

Foton World Fantasia

Markaz Al Bajja, As Seeb   24 537 061

Foton specialises in 'edutainment' for children, and this fun spot is a hit with kids of all ages. It has a climbing wall, games, bumper boats and Oman's first rollercoaster. Map 7 **2**

Magic Planet

Muscat City Centre, As Seeb   22 558 888

This amusement centre is popular with kids of all ages. Its main attractions include a small carousel, a mini train and bumper cars. Magic Planet has a party zone area that can be booked for private parties. For RO 30 you get an unlimited ride pass. Map 7 **3**

Naseem Park

Past Seeb Airport, As Seeb

This large park, opened in 1985, is on the highway leading to the Batinah area about 30km from Muscat International Airport. There is a train ride that goes round the park, a mini falaj (irrigation) system, a jasmine maze and well-tended Arabic and Japanese gardens, which were built to commemorate the strong ties between Japan and Oman. Map 7 **4**

Seeb Beach Park

Ar Rowdah St, Near Markhaz Al Bahja, As Seeb

Opened in 1997 on the lovely stretch of sandy beach, the Beach Park has invitingly clear waters, as well as a children's playground, to keep your tykes happy whatever their mood. Various watersports are available for adventurous guests. Map 7 **5**

Beach sunset

If you only do one thing in...
Al Seeb & Rusayl

Play on the rollercoaster at Foton World Fantasia (p.88); the only one in Oman.

Best for...

Eating and Drinking: The vast foodcourt in Markhaz Al Bahja (p.139) has something for everyone.

Sightseeing: Get yourself to Amouage (p.86), the most renowned perfume factory in the region.

Shopping: As Seeb is home to malls Muscat City Centre, (p.140) and Markaz Al Bahja (p.139), with tenants such as Marks & Spencer, Monsoon and Toys R Us to help you spend your hard-earned cash.

Relaxation: Seeb Beach Park (p.88) is good fun for all the family, with a playground for children and watersports for bigger kids.

Families: Magic Planet (p.88) amusement centre will wear out your kids in no time.

Clockwise from top left: Perfume, Local Crafts, Seeb City Centre

Oman Areas

Beyond Muscat, Oman boasts stunning scenery, lost cities, towering forts and unexpected lush greenery. Here is your guide to the rest of the country.

Al Dhahirah Region

Translated, Al Dhahirah means 'the back', aptly named since the region lies to the west of the Hajar Mountains, bordering the UAE and Saudi Arabia. The place is sparsely populated, due mainly to its sandy geography. In fact, there's not much in the way of modern-world comforts. Water is transported from the mountains to the towns using the age-old falaj (irrigation) system, which is deceptively sophisticated.

That said, this is an area where you'll see locals living their lives as they have done for centuries, and if you are fortunate you may get to see displays of traditional dances and crafts. It's also a great place for exploring old forts, ancient tombs and caves and is also home to the famous beehive tombs in Ibri (also called the Bat tombs).

Buraimi

The Buraimi governance falls on two borders. The one in Oman is called the Buraimi Oasis; the part on the UAE side is called Al Ain. Like Ibri, Buraimi can trace its history back to its strategic position at the intersection of various caravan routes to and from Oman. Being an oasis means this part of the country is pleasantly green with plenty of date palm plantations. It is a home to a famous mud fort, Hisn Al Khandaq, which has been extensively restored and is open to visitors. There is also a must-see camel souk where the merchants will happily explain the differences between one camel and another, and may even make a serious attempt at convincing you to buy one.

Ibri

Ibri lies between the foothills of the Hajar Mountains and the vast Rub Al Khali desert. With its central location, it was a historically important stopover for merchants travelling between the different regions of the Arabian Peninsula and trading remains active to this day. The bustling souk sells a range of merchandise, including locally produced woven palm goods. The most interesting sight though is the auction, which takes place every morning, where residents, farmers and traders from the town and surrounding villages come together to haggle over dates, fruit and vegetables, livestock, camels and honey.

Batinah Region

With a coastline stretching north-west from Muscat to the UAE border, Batinah has a collection of beautiful coastal towns and villages that are worth visiting. The most populated area after Muscat, Batinah has 12 wilayats (districts): Awabi, Barka, Khabura, Liwa, Musanaa, Nakhal, Rustaq, Saham, Shinas, Sohar, Swaiq and Wadi Mawail. Inland towards the western Hajars there are dramatic peaks and wadis.

Barka

Barka is a small coastal town west of Muscat. It makes for an interesting daytrip or as a stop off on a visit to Sohar, further along the coast. Famous for its fortnightly bullfights and large central fort, the place is still home to craftsmen practising traditional trades, including weaving. The historical fort, Bait Naa'man, and the Ostrich Breeding Farm are both attractions worth your time.

Nakhal

Only 30km inland from Barka and 100 kilometres from Muscat, Nakhal is definitely worth a quick trip, especially for its restored fort set on a hill. If you have the energy, climb to the top of the watchtowers to be rewarded with magnificent views of the surrounding countryside and town. Inside the fort, visitors can see the prison, kitchen, living quarters of the Wali (leader) and the male and female majlis. The area is also well known for the Al Thowarah hot springs. The natural spring water is channelled into the falaj system to irrigate the surrounding date plantations, and you can dip your toe in or have a paddle in the run-off water.

Rustaq

Once Oman's capital, Rustaq is today best known for Al Kersa Fort, a large and dramatic building extended over the years. Located in the western Hajar Mountains, about 170km south-west of Muscat, the areas has much to offer including a souk for visitors to explore. Not too far from here you'll find the hot springs for which Rustaq is famous. The water in these springs are believed to have healing powers – it has a high sulphur content, which is supposed to provide relief for sufferers of arthritis and rheumatism.

Sohar

Sohar lies about halfway between Muscat and Dubai, 200km north-west of the capital. Situated on the Batinah coast, it was once the maritime capital of the country. Sohar is renowned for its fort with an in-house museum (26 844 758), the lively Fish Souk (just off the corniche), and for being the birthplace of the legendary Sinbad the Sailor. To get to the fort take the city centre exit off the Muscat-Dubai highway, and after about two kilometres turn right at the second roundabout.

Dakhiliya Region

Despite being isolated from the sea, Dhakhiliya was historically important as many trade routes between the coast and the interior passed through the region. While you are in this part of the Sultanate, be sure to take your time and check out the various forts and ruins, namely the Bahla fort on Balhool Mountain and Jabrin Fort, where it is believed the Imam Bilarab (who built the place in the 1600s) is buried. While you're here you may as well nip to Bat and Al Ayn tombs, which date back to the third millennium BC.

Bahla

The ancient walled city of Bahla is only two hours' drive from Muscat, and just 40km from Nizwa. Though it has a small population, it still tallies 46 separate villages. While it is not yet on the mainstream tourist map, archaeology buffs and history enthusiasts will find it well worth a visit, since it is believed to be one of the oldest inhabited regions in Oman. In fact, archaeologists have found artefacts dating back to the third century BC here. Apart from its historical buildings, Bahla also has a rich and diverse ecology: a balanced mixture of fertile land, mountains, wadis and desert.

Nizwa

After driving deep into the Hajar Mountains, you'll find Nizwa, the largest city in Oman's interior. This oasis city offers fascinating sights and heritage, including Nizwa Fort (which dates back to the 17th century) and the magnificent Jabrin Fort, notable for its ceiling decorations and secret passageways. To get to the fort from Nizwa, follow the Ibri Road for about 45km and turn right at the signpost for Jabrin.

Sumail

The town of Sumail (or Samail) sits in the Sumail Gap, a natural valley that divides the Hajar Mountain chain into the eastern and western Hajars. As the most direct path between the coastal regions and the interior of the country, this route has always been an important artery. Irrigated by countless wadis and man-made falaj systems, the area is green and fertile. The dates produced here are highly rated.

Dhofar Region

Dhofar is the southernmost region of Oman, bordering Saudi Arabia and the Republic of Yemen. Dhofar frankincense is

Salalah

regarded as the finest in the world and once made this area immensely wealthy and important. Visitors still flock to the coast to enjoy the lush greenery and cool weather.

Salalah

Salalah, the capital of Dhofar, is home to museums and souks, all worthy of a trip. There are also many beautiful beaches to be found along the coast. The landscape features plenty of trees and lush greenery, thanks to its gentle climate, mainly at the border of the desert at the lower reaches of the jebels. Along the Yemen border is where the frankincense trees grow and are farmed by local villagers. They extract it by cutting into the trunks and allowing the sap to seep out and harden into lumps that are then scraped off and traded in bulk.

Ubar

At the crossroads of ancient trade routes, the Lost City of Ubar (referred to as Iram in the Quran) thrived as merchants came from far and wide to buy much sought-after incense. Traders converged to sell pottery, spices and fabric from India and China in return for the unique silver frankincense of Oman.

The commerce made Ubar a city of unrivalled wealth and splendour and those who visited it referred to it as 'paradise'. According to the Quran, the wickedness of the inhabitants led Allah to destroy the city and all roads leading to it, causing it to sink into the sand. For a thousand years the city's location remained unknown, until British explorer Sir Ranulph Fiennes, in a 20 year search using modern satellite technology, discovered the city beneath the shifting sands of the Omani desert near Shisr, north of Salalah.

Excavations have revealed the thick outer walls of a vast octagonal fortress with eight towers or pillars at its corners, and numerous pots and artefacts dating back thousands of years. Debate continues as to whether this is indeed Ubar, but the site is fascinating nonetheless and it was clearly an important desert settlement at one point. Tours of the city will take you through the Qara Mountains where you can enjoy the stunning landscape (see p.107).

Musandam Region

The Musandam peninsula is an Omani enclave to the north, which is divided from the rest of Oman by the United Arab Emirates. It is a beautiful, largely unspoiled area, only recently opened to tourists. The capital is Khasab, a quaint fishing port unchanged by the modern world. The Strait of Hormuz lies to the north, with Iran just across the water, the Arabian Gulf to the west and the Gulf of Oman to the east.

Musandam is dominated by the Hajar Mountains, which also run through the UAE and into the main part of Oman. It is sometimes referred to as the 'Norway of the Middle East', since the jagged mountain cliffs plunge directly into the sea, and the coastline features many inlets and fjords. The views along the coastal roads are stunning. Just a few metres off the coast you'll find beautiful and fertile coral beds, with an amazing variety of sea life including tropical fish, turtles, dolphins (a common sight) and, occasionally, sharks. Although the diving is not recommended for beginners, the more experienced will be in their element.

Inland, the scenery is equally breathtaking, although you will need a 4WD and a good head for heights to explore it properly. It is also advisable and much safer to travel in pairs when driving off-road.

Musandam's capital, Khasab, boasts the same stunning mountainous backdrop and is relatively spread out. Driving around, you will see it has numerous date palm plantations. There is a small souk and a beach, but the port is the main area of interest. At one end of the bay is the restored Khasab Fort, which is open to the public.

Bukha

Located on the western side of the Musandam peninsula, Bukha has its coastline on the Arabian Gulf. The small town is overlooked by the ruin of an old fort, but there is little to see other than the remains of one watchtower. The Bukha Fort is more impressive, however, and is on the side of the main road just metres from the sea. It was built in the 17th century, restored in 1990, and is certainly the town's biggest landmark.

Sharqiya Region

Sharqiya is a region of contrasts. The coastline features numerous fishing villages and ports, and the area's beaches are home to some of the most important turtle breeding grounds in the world. Inland, you'll find a combination of breathtaking wadis and dramatic expanses of sand dunes.

Masirah Island

Masirah Island lies 20km off the south-east coast of Oman and is the Sultanate's largest island. With hills in the centre and a circumference of picturesque isolated beaches, this is a hot destination for visitors and locals alike.

Sur

An old fishing and trading port 300km south-east of Muscat, Sur was famed for centuries for its boatbuilding and became quite prosperous as a result. Its fortunes did decline somewhat with the advent of more modern vessels and construction techniques, but Sur is enjoying something of a revival, and with its pretty corniche, forts and interesting Marine Museum, the town is definitely worth a visit. Take the time to visit the Sineslah Fort, which overlooks the town, and offers incredible views of the area and coast.

Jabrin Fort, Nizwa

Tiwi

Tiwi is a small fishing village up the coast from Sur, situated in a little cove between two of the most stunning wadis in the area: Wadi Tiwi and Wadi Shab. These verdant green oases are a must-see for anyone visiting the area, with their crystal clear pools and lush vegetation, including palm and banana plantations. The residents of Tiwi are spread across nine small villages and there are endless opportunities for walking and exploring. In Wadi Shab you can start your tour with a trip across the water, courtesy of a small boat operated by locals. Further along the wadi you can swim through pools and access a cave with a waterfall inside. Tiwi Beach, also known as the White Sands Beach, provides a tranquil spot for a rest.

Tours & Safaris

Whether you want to camp under the stars or clamber to Oman's highest peak, there is a tour for you.

Coastal Cruises

Coastal cruises are one of the best ways to make the very most of the extraordinary waters of Oman. A coastal cruise can be tailored to be as active or as languid as you like. Sail, dive, fish, snorkel, watch for dolphins, sunbathe and then indulge in some light refreshments as part of your package. There are two main spots to enjoy a coastal cruise: Marina Bander Al Rowdha (24 737288), on Oman's western coast and Moon Light Diving Centre (99 317700). Both have superb facilities and will happily customise your cruise.

Dolphin & Whale Watching

There are more than 20 species of whales and dolphins either living in or passing through the seas off the coast of Oman. While there's no guarantee of sightings, the odds are pretty high. Many tour operators will tentatively rate your chances of seeing dolphins at 85% to 90%. Whales are not so frequently seen – these gentle giants travel in smaller groups and stay under the surface for a lot longer, so you have to be a little bit more patient. Early mornings and evenings, when the seas are at their most calm, are the best times for sightings.

Saiq Plateau

Mosque Tours

Non-Muslims are not usually allowed inside mosques, but the Sultan Qaboos Grand Mosque allows visitors to admire its awesome Islamic architecture. Apart from being a place of worship, the building offers an insight into the cultural heritage of the Sultanate. With 263m of prayer carpet, 35 crystal chandeliers (the central one is 14 metres high and eight metres wide), and a floor entirely paved with marble, the interior will take your breath away. Tours are between 08:00 and 11:00 from Saturday to Wednesday. Dress conservatively.

Dune Dinner Safari

Escaping into the desert is an absolute must. Safaris are a fantastic way to unwind and enjoy the tranquility of the majestic dunes. Every tour operator will do things slightly differently, but generally you'll be driven inland towards the Hajar Mountains and then off-road through the lush green scenery and freshwater pools of Wadi Abyad. Then it's on to undulating dunes of the nearby Abyad desert for some exciting dune driving, before stopping to watch the sun set over the sands and a sumptuous barbecue.

Full-Day Safari

Perfect for desert lovers, this full-day adventure will have you exploring some of Oman's best attractions. You'll visit places such as the ruined fort of Mudairib, Shab village and the town of Sur. Some of the unforgettable sights you may see include traditional mud-brick homes clinging to steep valley walls, clear streams carrying fresh water into deep pools, and man-made irrigation systems (falaj). As you leave the mountains you'll head for the Wahiba Desert for an exhilarating ride over the dunes, some of which are 200m high.

Mountain Safari

The height and extent of Oman's mountain ranges are incredible . A trip into this part of the country will have you gazing up at the highest range, Jebel Akhdar, and up to Jebel Shams, which is Oman's highest peak at more than 3,000m. On the way, you'll pass through towns (such as Nizwa) and remote villages set on terraces cut into the mountains. From the top of Jebel Shams you'll see the awe-inspiring 'Grand Canyon' of Oman, a rocky canyon dropping thousands of metres from the plateau far below.

Overnight Turtle Watching

All tour operators offer trips to the famous Ras Al Jinz Turtle Sanctuary in Sur, where you can watch the rare sight of turtles coming onto the beach to lay their eggs. After arriving, you'll be served a beach barbecue before night falls and the turtles come lumbering onto the beach to lay their eggs and bury them in the sand. After a few hours sleep, you'll return to the beach and watch the mass of tiny hatchlings struggle out of their eggs and make their journey into the sea.

Wadi Drive

An off-road tour through the wadis can either be half-day, full-day or overnight, with camping in the peaceful surroundings of the rocky wilderness. You'll get to see falaj irrigation channels, in place for centuries, bringing water from underground springs to irrigate palm plantations and vegetable terraces. Natural streams run all year round in several wadis, transforming the dry, rocky landscape into fertile areas of greenery and clear rock pools that are often home to fish, frogs and other wildlife. Hidden villages in the mountains illustrate how people used to live.

Wahiba Desert

The Wahiba Desert stretches all the way from the coast to the mountains. This tour travels into the middle of seemingly endless dunes of red and white sand. Dune driving is a must-do; a ride up and down the steep slopes, courtesy of a very skilled driver, is like a natural rollercoaster. A visit to a traditional Bedouin homestead for Arabic coffee and dates follows, as does the chance to try camel riding, the oldest form of desert transport.

Overnight Desert Safari

Experience the peace of the desert for a night. After an exhilarating drive through the dunes you'll set up camp in a remote area of Wahiba, where Bedouin tribes have lived the old fashioned way for thousands of years.

At sunset, enjoy a camel ride while a barbecue is prepared and then relax under the starlit sky. In the morning, visit the flowing wadis to see the greenery and rugged mountain landscape, a complete contrast to the desert sights of the previous day.

East Salalah

Leaving Salalah and travelling east, this tour visits many historical sites and places of interest along the picturesque coast including the fishing village of Taqa, with its watchtowers and castle. Further on is Khor Rouri, a fresh-water creek now separated from the sea. This is the site of the ancient city of Samharam, known for its frankincense and for being the former capital of the Dhofar region. Also on the tour is the tomb of Mohammed bin Ali, the Ayn Razat ornamental gardens, the Hamran Water Springs and the historical trading centre of Mirbat.

West Salalah

Venture inland from Salalah to the northern part of the Qara Mountains, where the road winds up hairpin bends and eventually leads to the Yemen border. The tour goes to the tomb of the Prophet Job and the wadis and green pastures where they grow frankincense.

Returning from the mountains, you'll head to the spectacular Mughsail Beach where, at high tide, seawater gushes through natural blowholes in the limestone, reaching dizzying heights. On the way back to Salalah, visits will be made to the bird sanctuary and Mina Raysut.

Nizwa

This full-day tour explores the sights and heritage of this historically significant city, the third largest in Oman. After driving deep into the Hajar Mountains, the oasis city of Nizwa is home to the Nizwa Fort (which dates back to the

17th century) and the magnificent Jabrin Fort, notable for its wall and ceiling decorations and secret passageways. Many ancient ruins, such as Bahla Fort and mud-brick villages, can be seen among the date palm plantations and wadis.

Rustaq & Batinah

Batinah, the north-west region of Oman, has always been an important area for its abundant agriculture and strategic

Tour Operators

Organised tours are a great way to get out and explore. Ask at your hotel, which may be able to get you a special deal, or try one of the companies below.

Al Nimer Tourism	24 603 555
Arabian Sea Safaris	24 693 223
Bahwan Travel Agencies	24 704 455
Desert Discovery Tours	24 493 232
Eihab Travels	24 702 231
Empty Quarter Tours	99 387 654
Golden Oryx Tours	24 489 853
Grand Canyon of Oman Tours	92 605 102
Gulf Leisure	99 819 006
Gulf Ventures Oman	24 700 363
Hormuzline Tours Company	26 731 616
Khasab Travel & Tours	26 730 464
Mark Tours	24 562 444
Muscat Diving & Adventure Centre	24 485 663
Treasure Tours Land & Sea Adventure	99 349 399

Jebel Shams

position as the trading centre between the mountains and the coast. This area is home to many forts including the oldest and largest in the country, Al Kersa Fort. En route you will also visit the ancient souks, hot springs and sandy beaches, all amid spectacular mountain scenery.

Ubar

The discovery of the 'Lost City of Ubar' in the early 1990s caused great excitement in the archaeological world, when it was found that a huge limestone cavern underneath Ubar had collapsed, causing the city to sink into the sand. This full-day tour takes you through some stunning scenery as you drive through the Qara mountains to the site of this ancient city. Once the crossroads of significant trade routes, this was a place of unrivalled wealth and splendour – when Marco Polo visited Ubar he called it 'paradise'.

Further Out

If you've got the time, the United Arab Emirates are just a short flight or drive away, and are well worth a visit to complete your trip.

Abu Dhabi

Abu Dhabi is the capital of the UAE and is home to numerous luxury hotels, including one of the world's most expensive, Emirates Palace (www.emiratespalace.com). Abu Dhabi also offers a sprinkling of culture in the form of heritage sites and souks, as well as a selection of glistening new shopping malls.

Al Ain

Al Ain lies on the border with Oman and shares the Buraimi Oasis. The 'Garden City' offers many a pleasant stretch of rolling grassy plains, waterfalls and hot springs. Among the attractions in Al Ain are Hili Archaeological Garden, Al Ain Museum and the camel market. Jebel Hafeet, around 15km to the south of Al Ain, is a rather dramatic mountain that rises abruptly from the surrounding flat terrain and from which you have views over the desert and Al Ain.

Dubai

Dubai is the place to go if you're in need of a good night out or a new wardrobe. Renowned as the 'shopping capital of the Middle East', it boasts a number of large malls and a growing independent shopping scene. The city has a number of internationally respected restaurants and numerous bars and cafes. There's always something on in Dubai, from sporting events such as the Dubai World Cup and Dubai Tennis Championships to concerts, including the Jazz Festival and Desert Rock. You'll also find the traditional bustle of Deira Creek and the world-renowned Gold Souk. You can fly from Muscat International Airport to Dubai or Sharjah International Airports in about an hour. The straightforward drive will take closer to five hours, and involves crossing the Oman-UAE border near Hatta.

East Coast

A trip to the east coast of the UAE is worth the effort, especially as it's easy to get there from the Oman-UAE border near Hatta. The coast and the desert and mountains inland provide plenty of opportunities for sampling the great outdoors, from camping and off-road driving to snorkelling and scuba diving. The popular Snoopy Island is teeming with exotic marine life – including turtles and small sharks.

Liwa Oasis

A few hours south of Abu Dhabi by car lies Liwa Oasis, which is situated on the edge of the vast Rub Al Khali desert. It is also known as the Empty Quarter and is the largest sand desert in the world. If you appreciate spectacular scenery and enjoy a spot of camping, a trip into the dunes here is possibly one of the most rewarding experiences in the country. It is desolate and remote, but quite breathtaking and thoroughly recommended.

Sports & Spas

114 Sports & Activities
116 Watersports
120 Golf
124 Spas & Well-Being

Sports & Activities

Oman offers fantastic leisure options, from tranquil golf courses and spas to thrilling moonlit scuba diving – all in a stunning natural environment.

Consider this a land of opportunity when it comes to getting involved in sports and activities. The rugged mountains, unspoilt wadis, crystal clear sea and vast desert sands all make for breathtakingly beautiful surroundings in which to lose yourself in outdoor pursuits, particularly in the cooler months. Typically, residents spend their winter weekends camping on the beach, collecting shells and swimming. Weekends at the seaside are alternated with dune bashing on the sands at Wahiba, or a spot of sand skiing. Even the blistering heat of the summer doesn't stop avid sports enthusiasts from spending their leisure hours sailing the Gulf or hitting the golf courses.

You can't come here and not get up close and personal with a 'ship of the desert'. A lot of tour operators incorporate a quick camel ride as part of their desert safaris, and this is part of the experience of visiting the region. If you are more the spectator and are in Oman between April and August, you should get up early and head down to your nearest track between 06:00 and 09:00 to watch a camel race. You can find out more information about times and venues from one of the tour operators (see p.119).

If you're keen to get out and be at one with nature, you can always retreat to the stunning mountains for a spot of

Oman **mini** Explorer

Bike and hike Oman-style

camping, hiking, caving or off-road driving (see Explorer Publishing's Oman Off-Road for more information).

If you're longing for some cool when the summer heat hits 40°C and up, check out air-conditioned indoor activities such as bowling and ice skating. Try the City Bowling Centre in As Seeb (24 541 277), the Oman Bowling Centre in Al Khuwayr (24 480 747), or hit the ice in Al Khuwayr at the Ice Skating Centre (24 489 492) where you're sure to cool off. Alternatively, head south to the refreshingly rainy climes of Salalah where lower temperatures prevail.

Watersports

The myriad treasures of Oman's coastline are well worth exploring, be it by motor, sail, or under your own steam.

From canoeing to kayaking, jetskiing to coastal fishing, the waters off Oman are a veritable playground for water lovers. The geography of Oman's coastline, with underwater mountain ranges and drop offs of up to 300m or more, makes the sea life some of the most extraordinary you will find anywhere in the world.

Paddling allows you access to otherwise inaccessible places of natural beauty and provides unrivalled opportunities to get closer to the country's abundant bird and marine life.

Head north of Muscat and explore Musandam; you'll find unparalleled views of the spectacular fjord-like inlets and towering cliffs.

The Muscat Diving & Adventure Centre (see p.108) will rent you a kayak for half a day (with a guide) for a mere RO 40 per person, or RO 20 each for a group of four. Sailing and snorkelling are also great ways to appreciate above and below the sea with boat and yacht charters available.

Diving

It's the sheer quantity as well as the spectacular quality of Oman's sea life that makes this a hot diving destination. Get your flippers on and prepare yourself for a visual feast of turtles, cuttlefish, stingray, moray eels and more.

Colourful sealife

An attractive aspect of the warm waters of Oman is that you are likely to find a spot to suit everyone, whether novice or advanced. Cave diving and night diving are both unique and popular twists on underwater excursions.

If you've had previous experience then you'll need a diving permit from the ROP (Royal Oman Police) before getting under the sea. If you're a newbie, don't worry, you can have just as much fun with plenty of centres providing full training in PADI or BSAC, depending on what you're looking for. PADI's Open Water Certification is ideal if you're on holiday and just want to have a good splash about without too much delay.

Fahal Island in Muscat's Qurm region has around 10 dive sites, that offer good diving in most weather conditions. Diving depth is from three to 42 metres. Around Fahal Island are isolated reefs, a swim-through cave, and artificial reef balls. Non-divers will find good snorkelling on the western side of the island.

Bander Khayran is just 20 to 30 minutes away by boat or 40 minutes by 4WD from Muscat. This area consists of a small fjord system dotted with inlets. The diving depth ranges between one and 30 metres. It's known for diverse and beautiful corals and a wide variety of marine life.

Al-Munassir Naval Shipwreck, near Bander Khayran lies at a depth of about 30 metres. The rooms in the ship have been opened up for divers to go in and out of easily.

The nine Daymaniyat Islands span around 20 kilometres from Seeb to Barka. The islands and their surrounding reefs are a national nature reserve, and access is controlled. Thanks to this there is an extensive coral reef and abundant sea life.

Tour Operators & Dive Centres

Arabian Sea Safaris	www.arabianseasafaris.com
Shati Al Qurm, Muscat	24 693 223
Blu Zone Diving	www.bluzonediving.com
Sidab	24 737 293
Capital Area Yacht	
Sidab	24 737 712
Daymaniyat Divers	www.alsawadibeach.com
Barka	26 795 545
Global Scuba	www.global-scuba.com
MSQ , Muscat	24 692 346
Gulf Leisure	www.gulfleisure.com
Shati Al Qurm, Muscat	99 819 006
Hormuzline Tours Company	www.hormuzlinetours.com
Musandam	26 731 616
Khasab Travel & Tours	www.khasabtours.com
Musandam	26 730 464
Moon Light Diving Centre	www.moonlightdive.com
Shati Al Qur, Muscat	99 317 700
Musandam Extra Divers	www.musandam-diving.com
Musandam	26 730 501
Muscat Diving & Adventure Centre	www.holiday-in-oman.com
Al Khuwayr	24 485 663
Nomad Ocean	www.discovernomad.com
Dibba	971 50 885 3238
Oman Dive Centre	www.diveoman.com
Al Bustan	24 824 240

Sports & Spas

Watersports

Golf

Tee-off on Oman's speciality desert courses before enjoying a vibrant splash of green.

The lack of greenery has not been off-putting for the healthy number of supporters who play on 'brown' (sand) courses in Oman. However, all this is set to change with Muscat's first green golf course, Muscat Hills Golf & Country Club, due to open in 2009. Planned to be the region's preeminent course, the unique 18 hole tournament-grade landscape has been designed by top golf course designer David Thomas, and will combine Arabian wadis with verdant fairways and putting greens. The location is set to offer an academy, gated residential community, a hotel and a country club.

It's hoped this will boost the country's tourism sector and put the Sultanate on the golfing world map. Even without a green course in Muscat though, there are already several golf tournaments on Oman's annual calendar, including the Oman Ladies' Open Championship, the Men's Oman National Championship and the Ras al Ghala Trophy.

Those who haven't played golf in the Middle East before should be warned that the game here can be more physically demanding than elsewhere in the world – even acclimatised golfers avoid playing in the heat of the day during the summer months. And while the cool breezes of winter bring lower temperatures, it's always wise to carry plenty of drinking water and wear a sun hat.

Marco Polo Golf Course

Al Maha Golf Course   24 522 177
Oman Automobile Club, As Seeb

With two distinct seasons, April to September, and October to March, Al Maha offers a good range nearly year-round. Due to the intense heat in the summer months only nine holes are normally played and summer competitions are scheduled accordingly. The 18 hole season is played in winter. The club attracts a wide range of sponsors each year and is always looking for more competitive golfers. Coaching is available for beginners throughout the year.

Ghallah Wentworth Golf Club   24 591 248
Near As Sultan Qaboos Mosque, Ghala

This is a fair challenge for any level of player. The club has a driving range built on concrete tee boxes and a few sets of clubs for hire. Players should bring their own Astroturf mats for teeing off. There are two separate golf seasons; an 18 hole season in winter, and a nine hole season in summer, and competitions in these two categories are organised accordingly. Lessons are available upon request.

Marco Polo Golf Course   23 235 333
Crowne Plaza Resort, Salalah   www.crowneplaza.com

A relative newcomer on the Oman golfing scene, this is a grass course that includes a driving range, putting green and training area. The course itself is an unusual nine hole, par 3 that's set in a coconut grove. You can hire golf clubs if you wish, and even benefit from the assistance of a professional golf instructor on request.

Ghallah Wentworth Golf Club

Muscat Hills Golf & Country Club

24 510 065
www.muscatgolf.com

As Seeb

Muscat Hills Golf & Country Club will be carefully carved into the jebels, with great care taken to maintain the natural beauty of the surrounding landscape and wadis. An ambitious project aimed at superseding current courses in the Gulf, when completed in 2009 it is set to become the first 18 hole par 72 championship grass course in the Sultanate of Oman. A luxurious country club, academy, gated community and hotel will complement the course.

Spas & Well-Being

If you need more than just the soothing sounds of the sea to calm your soul, Oman offers personal indulgence on a platter.

Away from the souks and the dives, the camel riding and the belly-dancing, is another side of Oman, a decadent and pampering side that involves relaxing body and mind in luxurious locations. Health clubs and spas in the Sultanate offer a variety of ways to unwind, whether you need a deep muscle massage or a zingingly refreshing facial to perk you up, it's all here and packaged in sumptuously soothing style.

Al Jamal Health Club   24 490 526
Way 4429, Villa 2081, Al Azaiba

Al Jamal offers a range of body treatments, but specialises in Thai traditional massage for healthy bodies keen to keep them that way. It also does Thai, Indian oil, foot and facial massage. You can indulge in a full session of pampering by adding a Thai herbal and salt scrub or a herbal steam bath to your selection of treatments.

Al Kawakeb Ayurveda Clinic   24 494 762
Al Ghubbrah

Ayurveda aims to prevent disease through the use of herbs and natural therapies without fear of side-effects. All three branches of Al Kawakeb have separate treatment rooms for

CHI, The Spa at Shangri-La

men and women, where trained masseurs work under the supervision of experienced Ayurvedic consultants to provide the best of massages and herbal beauty care. Other locations: As Seeb 24 543 289; Al Qurm 24 564 101.

Al Nahda Resort & Spa
Barka

26 883 710
www.alnahdaresort.com

This new, luxurious resort and spa in Barka is a haven of pampering for weary souls in need of some care. Whether you want to improve your fitness, lose some of those extra pounds, or just spend a few days of blissful relaxation away from the stresses of everyday life, Al Nahda's expert team of fitness and health specialists will be able to help.

Ayana Slim Spa

24 693 435

Al Sarooj Plaza, Shati Al Qurm   www.ayanaspa.com

Looking and feeling good is taken to a whole new level at this spa. The Balinese-inspired decor with its water features and soft background music puts you in the mood for some serious pampering. You have a range of personalised spa treatments for body and hair to choose from (and they'll do wonders for your mind too). Massages range from Thai, Balinese and Swedish, through to crystal therapy.

The Spa Bar For Men

24 698 681

Jawharat A'Shati

An oasis for stressed-out businessmen, this is Oman's first and, to date, only spa dedicated to the male of the species. It offers a range of treatments, including soothing facials, manicures and pedicures so you'll walk out of this tranquil oasis feeling and looking like you're on top of your game.

The Spa

24 498 035

The Chedi Muscat, Al Ghubbrah   www.ghmhotels.com

Specialising in Balinese therapies, this luxurious spa at the Chedi is a temple of relaxation and serenity. You can easily spend an entire day being massaged, scrubbed, conditioned and polished. It also offers reflexology and Thai massage. Speciality therapies are also available, such as the Ocean Ritual and The Omani Bliss Ritual. Enjoy individual treatments or spoil yourself completely with a spa package (and yes, bookings are essential).

Shopping

130 Shop Oman
134 Hotspots
138 Shopping Malls
142 Souks & Markets
146 Where To Go For...

Shop Oman

Head for Oman's many colourful souks for those regional must-haves, or hit the malls for global brands and boutique surprises.

Muscat is the shopping capital of Oman. It offers a cosmopolitan range of stores, from boutiques to handicraft stalls, but it's the lively and authentic markets (souks) that really capture the imagination.

Distinguished old men in their dishdashas sit behind the counters presiding over their goods, while bejewelled women in their abayas haggle with vendors. Every important town in Oman has at least one souk.

The biggest and most famous of these are in Mutrah, Nizwa, Sinaw and Salalah and there's a women-only souk in Ibra every Wednesday morning. In addition to the permanent souks, pre-Eid markets known as 'habta' souks spring up overnight in places such as Fanja, Samayil, Suroor, Nafa'a and Nizwa.

Check out Al Dhalam Market in Mutrah for Arabian atmosphere, gold, silver and spices. You should dress respectfully and appropriately (this is old-school Arabia where modesty is a must and cameras are best left behind). The Gold Souk in Salalah brings a little bling to your life, while Mutrah Souk is considered one of the most interesting in the region, with warren-like covered stalls, all still family-owned and run, selling a mishmash of household supplies and traditional souvenirs. The layout is confusing but getting

Gold and gifts

lost is the best part. Nizwa Souk has a little bit of everything, from silver to fish, and the handicrafts of every region of Oman. Visit the fish and vegetable souk in Muscat for one of the city's more eye-opening and nostril-filled shopping and cultural diversions.

It's all tax-free shopping, which may ease the guilt of forking out your rials faster then you can say 'wrap it up'.

Modern shopping centres, replete with global brands and ample parking, are pivotal social settings. Wednesday, Thursday and Friday nights are the busiest shopping times, and it can get a little too crowded, even for the serious shopper. During Ramadan some shops are open until midnight, supermarkets are packed to the brim with unbelievable amounts of food, and the queues are long, especially in the evenings. Many shops have sales during the annual Muscat Festival in January.

Outside of the souks or the shops in Ruwi, bargaining is less common and involves more subtle hinting than overt haggling.

Shop & Ship

Thanks to the varied choice of local treasures and shopping pleasures you may find that your purchases exceed your luggage allowance. Luckily, you don't have to curb your shopping spree as you can just ship. You will pay by the kilo and rates vary, try Aramex (24 563 668, www.aramex. com), DHL (24 563 599, www.dhl.com), or one of the other major shipping or courier companies listed in the Omantel telephone directory.

Khanjars

Hotspots

Away from Muscat's air-conditioned malls there is plenty to explore. Here are some of Oman's alternative retail gems.

Capital Store
24 561 888

Various Locations

Capital Store is the ultimate shopping destination if you like luxury, and lots of it. This is where to head if you're looking for a Mont Blanc watch or pen, branded luggage, Dior sunglasses, or jewellery by Misaki and Nina Ricci. Capital also stocks a fantastic range of crystal and china, tableware, appliances and homewares, as well as one of Oman's widest ranges of perfumes and cosmetics.

Khimji's Megastore
24 796 161

Various Locations

Megastore in this case doesn't mean vast: it means mega-exclusive. The fact that you have to be buzzed in to enter is quite understandable once you see the brands lining the walls of this chrome and marble store. It's a who's who of well known upmarket names such as Channel, Jaeger, Paco Rabanne, Samsonite, OshKosh and Cross, to namedrop but a few. The watch department boasts some of the world's finest timepieces, including Rolex and Cartier, so bring your credit card. Other brands include Bulgari, FCUK, Nikon, Nina Ricci, Ralph Lauren, Ray-Ban and Swarovski.

Salman Stores   24 560 135
Various Locations

Salman Stores was founded in 1953 as a retailer of quality kitchen and home products. Some 50 years on, the group has grown into a leading importer, distributor and retailer in Oman and its range of products has expanded dramatically. This is the place to go if you're looking for tableware, glass and crystal items, porcelain and china, cutlery, and electrical appliances. Salman also stocks a range of luxurious linen and luggage. It has branches in Capital Commercial Centre (24 560 135), Al-Araimi Complex (24 566 286), Mutrah (24 796 925), Seeb (24 422 213) and Salalah (23 293 146).

Nizwa

Nizwa is a great place for souvenir shopping. This atmospheric, historical town is just a 90 minute drive from Muscat, and once there it's easy to find your way around. Getting there involves a fabulously scenic drive, with breathtaking mountains all the way. Particularly worth checking out is the souk. The people here call themselves the 'real Omanis' and pride themselves on being friendly and helpful. The pace of life is much slower here and a day trip is a relaxing break from Muscat's hustle and bustle.

Ruwi Souk Street

Better known as Ruwi High Street, this is a very long, double-laned street that starts at the Al Hamriya Roundabout. It's the place to go for anything from toilet seats to diamond rings, state-of-the-art Hi-Fi systems to Delsey luggage and every thing else in between. While most of the shops cater to lower-income families, expats of all nationalities come here for the excellent and inexpensive picture framing shops and tailors, and to buy textiles, appliances and gold.

Salalah

It may well be Oman's second biggest city but Salalah still manages to retain that small village feeling. With this in mind, don't expect to find the same range and variety of shops as in Muscat, but do indulge in the bargain hunting to be had, particularly for perfume, incense, oils and incense burners. The Al Husn Souk (next to the Palace) is particularly good for silverware, frankincense and locally made perfume. Incense remains quite big business in Dhofar and entire alleys of the Salalah souk are devoted to incense shops

While there aren't really any shopping malls as such, Salalah does excel in the street lined shops that sell clothes, textiles, groceries, appliances and stationery. The length of Al Haffa Street is packed with small stores selling mainly women's clothes and accessories. Dhofar City Centre has a little bit of everything under one roof, but sells mainly clothes and accessories for the whole family. Salalah's semi-tropical climate supplies Oman with fresh produce such as bananas, coconuts, tomatoes, and beans. Locally grown foods are cheap and bountiful. Look out for the small stalls along the beaches or back streets where you can buy finger-sized sweet bananas straight off the trees and drink milk right out of the coconut.

Local flavour and spices

Shopping Malls

Shop, browse, meet, drink and socialise;
a mall in Oman is for so much more
than shopping.

Al-Araimi Complex
Al Qurm, Muscat   24 566 180

This nifty little mall boasts more than 70 stores jam packed
full of fashion, electronics, homewares. There's an Oman
Mobile shop and several photo shops, including PhotoMagic
and Photocentre. It also has its very own (and very handy)
branch of the National Bank of Oman.

Al Harthy Complex
Al Qurm   24 564 481

This standalone building beside the bustling Sultan Center
looks like a cross between a space rocket and a futuristic
mosque. The mall is an impressive landmark, especially at
night when the lattice roof and the blue dome are lit up. It's
less harried than some of the other shopping locations and
has a nice internet cafe and cool little eateries. Look out for
The Gallery, where you'll find the works of prominent Omani
artists on display.

Captial Commercial Centre (CCC)
Al Qurm   24 563 672

Looking like a sprawling Omani fort, complete with flags
and enormous, carved wooden doors, CCC is an incredible

gathering of stores. There's loads in here, from the Canadian coffee shop chain, Second Cup, serving up frothy lattes, to the Al Fair Supermarket. The shopping centre also has a good array of jewellery, phone, carpet and perfume shops under a beautiful stained glass ceiling.

Jawaharat A'Shati
Shati Al Qurm   24 692 113

All manner of 'stuff' is sold here from hand-rolled cigars to Turkish icecream and Italian coffee. Make time to browse around The Oman Heritage Gallery, it's like spending the day in a museum and you get to pick up some beautiful knick-knacks, all made by local artists. Hidden behind red and pink glass walls is Nails, Muscat's only salon devoted to beautifying your talons with the addition of a new Spa Bar for men.

Landmark Group (City Plaza)
Near Al Khuwayr Roundabout, Al Khuwayr   24 698 988

More of a department store than a mall, this big two-storey building is a very popular destination and home to all manner of stores catering to all tastes and budgets, from baby clothes to homeware and everything in between.

Markaz Al Bahja
As Seeb   24 541 952

This place is huge and still a little on the quiet side, but that's sure to change as it starts to shed its new kid on the block reputation. It's a little further out of town and closer to Seeb but well worth the trip for some good shopping. Many of the clothes shops specialise in traditional Omani dress. However, Marks & Spencer, Toys R Us and ID Design are all big attractions in the Markaz, as is the vast foodcourt and the regular family entertainment on offer. The basement has an eight-lane bowling alley, complete with billiards and internet cafe.

Muscat City Centre
As Seeb   24 558 888

So far this is the biggest, busiest and most modern of all the malls in the Sultanate. Although French hypermarket Carrefour, where you can find everything from a flat-screen TV to beauty products, takes up a good chunk of space, the rest of City Centre is jam packed with good options, including numerous brand fashion stores, jewellery shops, eateries and coffee stops where you can recharge before hitting the next section.

Sabco Commercial Centre
Al Qurm   24 566 701

This was one of the first real shopping malls in Oman, and while some may prefer the glitz and glamour of the newer malls, Sabco retains a loyal following of shoppers. It's normally relatively quiet so shopping here is actually a relaxing experience, made even more so by the gardens and indoor waterfalls. There are plenty of wooden benches for a quick rest when you've exhausted yourself after a marathon spending session.

Treasures of Mutrah Souk

Souks & Markets

For a very real slice of the Middle East, make it a priority to visit the souks and markets of Oman.

Al Dhalam Market
Near Al Lawatiya Mosque, Mutrah, Muscat

Al Dhalam means 'darkness', an appropriate name for this area since the narrow alleyways receive little sunlight. When the market was originally built from mud and barasti, shoppers used lamps to find their way around. It's since been modernised – well, a little – and at least has paved alleyways and lanterns on the walls to light the way. The Al Lawatiya quarter was previously closed to foreigners (even non-Lawati Muslims). However, now you are free to wander around to your heart's content, browsing through the silver jewellery, traditional Omani ornaments, textiles and spices. Please note that you should dress appropriately (this is an area where modesty is required), and leave your camera behind.

Gold Souk
Salalah Centre, Salalah

People unfamiliar with Arabic gold may think it is of a poorer quality, but the reverse is actually true. Most of the gold sold in the region is 24 carat, and often softer and better quality than gold bought elsewhere in the world. However, it is very yellow and you may find that the designs are a bit gaudy, depending on your tastes. A visit to the Salalah Gold Souk

will still be a breathtaking if not blinding experience. You can shop around for a traditional Dhofari design, or design your own piece and have it made. This souk shouldn't be confused with the gold souk in Souk Al Haffa – the Salalah Gold Souk is in the Salalah Centre (after Pizza Hut turn right 50 metres before the traffic lights).

Mutrah Fish & Vegetable Market
Near Fish Roundabout, Mutrah, Muscat

The fish market at the Mutrah end of the Corniche is one of the few places in Muscat where you can still bear witness to the real hustle and bustle of an Arabic market. Smelly, muddy and bloody, it's an unforgettable experience and one best sampled by those with a strong constitution. It's also the best place to buy fresh seafood at low prices, but you'll have to get there early to score the catch of the day. On the left of the fish market is a very good fruit and vegetable section. The wide variety of locally grown and imported produce is cheap, especially considering the huge quantities you can buy. At the entrance to the vegetable market is a row of meat shops selling fresh cuts of beef, mutton and camel.

Mutrah Souk
Mutrah Corniche, Mutrah, Muscat

One of the most interesting souks in the Gulf, this warren-like covered market is still a source of many Omani families' daily household supplies, as well as a hotspot for souvenir-hunting tourists. The main thoroughfare carries primarily household goods, shoes and ready-made garments. Further inside, you can enjoy the mixed scent of frankincense, perfume oils, fresh jasmine and spices. The real excitement lies in exploring the side streets. The layout is confusing, but keep walking and you'll end up somewhere fun. Wander down any of the side alleys and you'll discover a selection of tiny shops full of dusty Omani silver, stalls of gleaming white dishdashas and embroidered kumahs, multi-coloured head scarves, Omani pots, paintings, hookah pipes, framed khanjars, leatherwork and incense. There are plenty of bargains and no price is fixed, so haggle, haggle and then haggle some more. When you get tired, you can stop at the juice bar before tackling the next section.

Nizwa Souk
Town Centre, Nizwa

In the centre of Nizwa, close to the fort and mosque, this gem lies hidden behind imposing sand-coloured walls. Enter through one of the enormous carved wooden doors and you'll find a small village of traditionally designed buildings. Each labelled to indicate the products they sell – Silver Souk, Fish Souk, Meat Souk and so on. Although these buildings are all clean, well lit and renovated, the place remains full of atmosphere and traders conduct business as they have done for centuries. The souks are well laid out and vibrant with local colour, especially in the early morning. The shop owners are an unobtrusive bunch and are happy to sit and drink coffee while you browse. Although prices are rising as tourism increases, with hard bargaining you can sometimes get a better price than in Muscat.

Where To Go For...

Silver

The bling factor of Oman is massively heightened by its reputation for high-quality silverware. Not just used for jewellery, silver is popular in decorating weapons as well as making everyday objects like coffee pots and pipes. Each region in the Sultanate has its own distinctive design. Don't be put off by the blackened and dusty bits of beauty – there is nothing that a bit of polish can't fix. Seek and ye shall find some real treasures.

Textiles

Oman is a haven for textile lovers with an array of fabric, textures, prices, colours and prints. Even the smallest towns will have fabric stores so shop to your heart's (and wallet's) content. Surprisingly, cotton isn't very big in the Arab world but silk and linen are plentiful. Look out for beautiful Indian printed cushion covers and bed spreads that are bound to bring a touch of the exotic to your daily life.

Perfume

Strong heady smells tend to dominate much of Oman and pure frankincense, jasmine and musk actually originated from this very region. The souks are a fabulous place to find the perfect scent with hundreds of fragrances vying for your attention. Be careful, some of the purer stuff is super strong and a drop or two on your scarf can last for a few days. Oudh is highly valued in the Middle East and can fetch astonishing prices. Made from the resin of Aloeswood trees and imported from India, Cambodia and Malaysia, Oudh is worn on clothes and skin and usually only on important occasions. Amouage is said to be 'the world's most valuable perfume' and is made here in Oman. You can visit the Amouage factory (p.86) in Rusayl, past Seeb.

Carpets

Camel or goat hair, sheep wool or cotton, dyed, weaved, patterned or still in their natural states, weaving is one of Oman's major handicrafts and the skill is still passed down through generations. Carpet shopping can be an absolute minefield so have a set budget and know what size you're after. The carpet's origin, intricacy of design, its material and whether it is machine made or hand-woven will all dictate its value. Hand-woven products tend to have more imperfections but this actually increases its value. Haggling is expected and encouraged.

Souvenirs

Traditional Arabic gear makes for the best presents and a lot of the stuff you'll find is made in and around Oman. If you want nothing but the real thing, head down to the Oman Heritage Gallery, near the InterContinental Hotel Muscat. This government-run shop sells only genuine crafted items. Incense burners, khanjar daggers, perfume and frankincense all make excellent gifts to take back home, as does silverware.

Going Out

150 Omani Eats
152 Venue Directory
154 Qurm & Qurm Heights
158 Shati Qurm
164 Ruwi
166 Al Bustan, Sidab & Qantab
170 Madinat Sultan Qaboos
172 Al Khuwayr
174 Al Ghubbrah

Omani Eats

Whether it's fine dining or a quick pit stop while out shopping, Oman's culinary spread will satisfy your appetite without busting your wallet.

With plenty of beaches, a stunning backdrop of mountains and year-round good weather, Oman is a fantastic place to explore. However, if you love late-night partying at glamorous clubs, sipping elegant cocktails at trendy bars or enjoying modern cuisine prepared by celebrity chefs, you might find the nation's nightlife somewhat limited. That said, Muscat's five-star hotels still offer some excellent fine-dining restaurants.

This chapter focuses on Muscat because this is where you'll find the greatest choice of cafes, restaurants and bars. An array of international cuisine can be found in the city's five-star hotels (p.32). The Chedi Muscat (p.35) and The Shangri-La's three hotels (p.34) offer some of the best options. The city also boasts a number of cheaper independent places, both Arabic and Indian, that are worth your attention.

Although Oman is a Muslim country, independent restaurants are permitted to apply for a licence to serve alcohol. That said, there's quite a hefty mark-up on drinks, with a decent bottle of wine often costing as much as your meal.

On p.151 there's a quick reference listing that will help you find precisely the right spot, depending on your mood and the occasion.

Local ingredients

Venue Directory

Whether you feel like cocktails or coffee, a table under the stars or a taste of local cuisine, below is the best Oman has to offer.

Alfresco		
Al Bustan	Seblat Al Bustan	p.169
Al Bustan, Sidab & Qantab	Bait Al Bahr	p.167
Al Khuwayr	Fish Village	p.173
Muscat	Chedi Poolside Cabana	p.174
Qurm & Qurm Heights	Club Safari Rooftop & Grill	p.156
Shati Al Qurm	Marjan Poolside Restaurant	p.161
Shati Al Qurm	Sirj Tea Lounge	p.159
Shati Al Qurm	Tomato	p.152
Breakfast		
Qurm & Qurm Heights	Marina Café	p.155
Shati Al Qurm	D' Arcy's Kitchen	p.159
Shati Al Qurm	Le Mermaid Cafe	p.159
Shati Al Qurm	Mussandam Cafe and Terrace	p.161
Buffets		
Al Bustan, Sidab & Qantab	Al Tanoor	p.166
Al Bustan, Sidab & Qantab	Samba	p.168
Al Khuwayr	Olivios Coffee Shop	p.173
Qurm & Qurm Heights	Tropicana	p.157
Ruwi	Green Mountain	p.165
Casual		
Al Khuwayr	Alauddin Restaurant	p.172
Qurm & Qurm Heights	Bollywood Chaat	p.155

Qurm & Qurm Heights	Duke's Bar	p.157
Ruwi	Golden Oryx	p.164
Ruwi	Woodlands	p.165
Cocktails		
Al Ghubbrah	The Lobby Lounge	p.175
Shati Al Qurm	Club Safari	p.163
Shati Al Qurm	Senor Pico's	p.161
Shati Al Qurm	Trader Vic's	p.162
Kids Welcome		
Al Ghubbrah	Al Mas Brasserie	p.174
MSQ	Al Madina	p.170
Qurm & Qurm Heights	Automatic	p.155
Qurm & Qurm Heights	Cafe Glacier	p.154
Qurm & Qurm Heights	Marina Café	p.155
Live Music		
Al Bustan, Sidab & Qantab	The Piano Lounge	p.169
Ruwi	Uptown	p.165
Shati Al Qurm	Al Ghazal Pub	p.163
Shati Al Qurm	Copacabana	p.163
Shati Al Qurm	O Sole Mio	p.161
Local Cuisine		
Al Khuwayr	Bin Ateeq	p.172
Al Khuwayr	Ofair Public Foods	p.173
Reservations Recommended		
Al Bustan	Beach Pavilion	p.167
Al Bustan	China Mood	p.168
Al Bustan, Sidab & Qantab	Capri Court	p.168
Shati Al Qurm	Tuscany	p.162

Qurm & Qurm Heights

This part of town has it all: excellent beaches, fabulous shopping and the most tantalising eateries.

Venue Finder

Cafe	Café Glacier	p.154
Cafe	Marina Café	p.155
Arabic/Lebanese	Automatic	p.155
Chinese	China Town	p.156
Chinese	Silk Route	p.157
Indian	Bollywood Chaat	p.155
Indian	Mumtaz Mahal	p.156
International	Tropicana	p.157
Persian	Shiraz	p.156
Steakhouse	Club Safari Rooftop Grill	p.156
Pub	Duke's Bar	p.157

Cafes

Café Glacier

CCC Complex   24 489 245

This cafe serves as a welcome retail pit stop. Well-presented dishes and generous portions satisfy a hungry crowd. Free popcorn will appeal to the kids, and high chairs are available. As well as the coffee, there are herbal teas, fruit smoothies and a menu that includes breakfasts, pasta, salads, soups, sandwiches and pancakes, all served by efficient waiting staff.

Marina Café

Near Crowne Plaza 24 567 825

This is a great place on the Shati beachfront with some of the best views in the city. The architecture is contemporary, and with curved walls leading into a cool and comfortable cafe, or up to the next floor where you can eat under the stars. Serving seafood and salads, snacks and juices, the Marina Café is popular with both locals and expats.

Restaurants

Automatic

Arabic/Lebanese

Near Sabco Centre 24 561 500

Automatic has established itself as the benchmark for fast Arabic food. It's all about fresh juices, mezze and large portions at very reasonable prices. Those with large appetites will love the four daily specials, while the range of traditional starters, salads, grilled meats and locally caught seafood ensures that everyone can find something they enjoy.

Bollywood Chaat

Indian

CCC Complex 24 565 653

This is a vegetarian restaurant with a Bollywood-themed menu of light meals and snacks, in a bright and pleasant setting. The heart-shaped potato cutlets (kajol cutlet) and the sweet and sticky dumplings (moon moon gulab jamun) are two dishes you shouldn't miss. The fact that everything is so reasonably priced makes a meal at Bollywood that little bit more special.

China Town
CCC Complex

Chinese
24 567 974

Much-loved and well-known dishes are served in a serene setting, and expectations of fabulous fare are well met. A takeaway and delivery service is also available, but those dining in will enjoy excellent food presented in a 'no-fuss' manner by friendly and courteous staff.

Club Safari Rooftop Grill
Grand Hyatt

Steakhouse
24 641 234

With a spectacular backdrop of the sea, and overlooking the pool, the Rooftop Grill is only open during the cooler months (October to May) to allow diners to make the most of the view. As the name would suggest, dishes range from steaks to lobster, all grilled. There are also fresh salads, assorted side-dishes, soups and a range of desserts.

Mumtaz Mahal
Near Qurm National Park

Indian
24 605 907

Costumed waiters will ply you with baskets of poppadoms and dips while you make your choice. During the peak season a traditional Indian band plays, adding to a lively and relaxed atmosphere. The restaurant has a great vantage point overlooking Qurm National Park.

Shiraz
Crowne Plaza

Persian
24 660 660

A tented ceiling and open bread preparation area add to the already-plush setting at this Persian gem. It is definitely advisable to take along a huge appetite for the generous, and complimentary, portions of cheese, salad and Arabic bread you get before your meal. The starters are a particular treat – you could just order a mountain and forgo the mains.

Silk Route   Chinese
Near Sabco Centre   24 561 741

Silk Route draws fans from both the local and expat communities and is really busy in the evenings, particularly at the weekend. You'll find a varied menu of Chinese, Cantonese and Szechwan cuisines, including delicious dim sum.

Tropicana   International
Crowne Plaza   24 660 660

With an international menu ranging from Indian and Mediterranean dishes to the classic American burger, and theme nights on Wednesdays and Thursdays, this place covers all bases. Lunchtime means a loaded buffet. The poolside location offers a pleasant alfresco option.

Pub

Duke's Bar
Crowne Plaza   24 660 660

Simple bar food, executed with excellence. Starters, such as the veal and turkey pate, could pass for fine cuisine, while the main courses are accompanied by crunchy fresh vegetables and delicious sauces. Service is swift and drinks flow freely. There's also quiz nights and live music.

Shati Al Qurm

This neighbourhood is the epitome of luxury, so expect your dining experience to be decadent.

Venue Finder

Cafe	D'Arcy's Kitchen	p.159
Cafe	Le Mermaid Cafe	p.159
Cafe	Sirj Tea Lounge	p.159
Arabic/Lebanese	Al Barouk	p.160
Arabic/Lebanese	Al Deyar	p.160
Far Eastern	Far Eastern Restaurant	p.160
Far Eastern	Marjan Poolside Restaurant	p.161
Italian	O Sole Mio	p.161
Italian	Tuscany	p.162
Mediterranean	Musandam Cafe & Terrace	p.161
Mediterranean	Tomato	p.162
Mexican	Senor Pico's	p.161
Polynesian	Trader Vic's	p.162
Bar	Club Safari	p.163
Pub	Al Ghazal Pub	p.163
Nightclub	Copacabana	p.163

Cafes

D'Arcy's Kitchen

Jawharat A'Shati   24 600 234

Overlooking the sea, this sunny cafe in the buzzing Shati Al
Qurm area welcomes you in for a late breakfast, lunch or a
light dinner. Once inside, you'll feel as though you've stepped
into a farmhouse kitchen and the theme is matched by the
hearty servings. The menu includes special salads, soups and
burgers served with a selection of delicious fruit smoothies.

Le Mermaid Cafe

Near Grand Hyatt   24 602 327

This is one of the coolest cafes in Muscat. With a large outside
seating area and great sea views, majlis tents and shisha,
this popular spot has people buzzing all over town. Dishing
up a wide range of seafood, grills and snacks, Le Mermaid
is a hidden treasure. Indulge in a refreshing fruit cocktail or
choose from the range of coffees and local hot drinks.

Sirj Tea Lounge

Grand Hyatt   24 641 234

Comfortably furnished in Arabian style, the Sirj Tea Lounge
offers you the choice of taking your tea in a tented or open
area. Their traditional English afternoon tea consists of finger
sandwiches, homemade scones with clotted cream and jam,
and a large slice of the cake of your choice. You may be lucky
enough to have the resident pianist treat you to light music
while you sip away your afternoon.

Restaurants

Al Barouk
Arabic/Lebanese

Beach Hotel
24 604 799

The interior is simple yet thoughtfully decorated and the atmosphere conducive to a relaxed meal. A Lebanese musician and singer play gentle tunes on Monday nights. If you want to dine alfresco, the best spot is by the hotel pool – perfect for relaxing, taking in the view and enjoying some shisha. Al Barouk is licensed to serve alcohol.

Al Deyar
Arabic/Lebanese

Near Shati Cinema
24 603 553

Bizarrely sculpted concrete on the walls and suspended mats on the ceiling give this place a kind of surreal stage appearance, and you could read all sorts of symbolism into the till's novel placement upon a fish tank. The great thing about Al Deyar is its ample outdoor seating – perfect for shisha and lapping up the sea breeze.

Far Eastern Restaurant
Far Eastern

Sheraton Qurm
24 605 945

Though it misses out on a sea view, the food here is well worth your full attention. Choose your meal from a selection of Chinese, Thai or teppanyaki dishes and all the takeaway classics, including lemon chicken and seafood noodles. The typical Oriental puddings, from lychees to delicious icecreams, are fabulously indulgent. Thursday sushi nights always attract the crowds.

Marjan Poolside Restaurant

Far Eastern

Grand Hyatt

24 641 234

Set to the side of a beach that overlooks the Arabian Gulf, the Marjan Poolside Restaurant is in a beautifully landscaped garden courtyard. The real treat is the fact that you get to select your fish, decide how it should be cooked – grilled, fried or steamed in banana leaf – and then pick your sauces before settling down to a superb meal.

Musandam Cafe & Terrace

Mediterranean

Hotel InterContinental

24 680 000

This is the ultimate spot for a Friday family brunch. The vast buffet includes breakfast classics, as well as fresh fish, roast meats and salads. Little ones can have their faces painted and watch magic shows, leaving you with your hands free to pile up your plate. Breakfast, lunch and dinner are also served.

O Sole Mio

Italian

Jawharat A'Shati

24 601 343

An award-winning restaurant, this place is ideal for a candlelit dinner for two or an informal dinner with friends, thanks to its lively atmosphere, musical entertainment and delicious Italian fare. The menu is extensive, with plenty of grilled options for the health conscious, and servings are ample.

Senor Pico's

Mexican

Hotel InterContinental

24 680 000

Start with a margarita and wake up your tastebuds with a hefty dose of jalapeno (which you'll find hidden in the complimentary dips). All the favourites are here: burritos, fajitas, enchiladas, a mean chilli con carne, and must-try nachos. Portions are ample and so is the price tag, so save those sour-cream calories for special occasions.

Tomato
Hotel InterContinental

Mediterranean
24 680 000

All tables are located on a deck and you can't dine inside, so this is a venue best when the weather isn't too sticky. The food is the perfect combination of simple, wholesome classics and innovative flavours, and the funky cutlery and dazzling range of crockery wouldn't be out of place in any cutting-edge European eatery.

Trader Vic's
Hotel InterContinental

Polynesian
24 680 000

Notorious for its colourful cocktails and live Cuban music, Trader Vic's also boasts a vibrant menu to spice up your evening. A sushi menu is served from a gigantic clamshell or choose from curries, stir-fries or crispy duck pancakes.

Tuscany
Grand Hyatt

Italian
24 641 234

The menu is extensive and offers all the classic Italian dishes. If your favourite isn't there, just ask the chef and he'll oblige. The food is superb and the service impeccable. Tuscany maintains that perfect blend of formal dining with a relaxed atmosphere – and it is clearly sought after, so be sure to reserve a table.

Bars & Pubs

Al Ghazal Pub
Hotel InterContinental   24 600 500

Rock up for a traditional pub experience that is second
to none. With a friendly atmosphere, a huge selection of
beverages, delicious pub fare and live entertainment, what
more could you want? Diners can tuck into steak, fish and
chips, or just a light sandwich, from the menu.

Club Safari
Grand Hyatt   24 641 234

Faux animal skins, African masks and bamboo adorn the walls
and ceiling creating an atmosphere that's over-the-top but
kind of appealing. The Safari Pub, on the middle level of this
three floor extravaganza, has a distinct party atmosphere and
regulars range from sports fans, who come for the multitude
of TV screens, to party princesses who strut their stuff and sip
the (not cheap) exotic cocktails.

Nightclub

Copacabana
Grand Hyatt   Nightclub
                                                24 641 234

One of the liveliest nightclubs in Muscat – especially if people-
watching is high on your agenda. The music is an eclectic mix
of the good, the bad and the ugly, and features anything that
hit the playlists in the last 15 years. Local males dominate the
dancefloor, even if couples are the target clientele.

Ruwi

Though predominantly business oriented, the dining in this part of town is still worth your attention.

Venue Finder

Chinese	Golden Oryx	p.164
Filipino	Palayok Restaurant	p.165
Indian	Copper Chimney	p.164
Indian	Woodlands	p.165
International	Green Mountain	p.165
Bar	Uptown	p.165

Restaurants

Copper Chimney
CBD Area

Indian
24 706 420

Behind the impressive copper doors lies an equally striking interior. The fine Indian fare served within perfectly meets the expectations that the decor raises. Take a table under the high, domed ceiling, complete with great copper lamps or watch your meal being prepared in the vast clay oven.

Golden Oryx
Opposite Bank of Muscat

Chinese
24 702 266

Golden Oryx has been serving up delicious Far Eastern cuisine for 25 years. Aside from the menu, featuring authentic Chinese cuisine and some delicious Thai delicacies, Golden Oryx also offers an excellent Mongolian barbecue.

Green Mountain
Sheraton Oman

International
24 799 899

Green Mountain's formal exterior – rather reminiscent of a 1970s Dallas skyscraper – doesn't hint at the laidback, all-you-can-eat buffet that lies within, but it's definitely there. An international buffet keeps diners happy throughout the week.

Woodlands
Near Europcar Building

Indian
24 700 192

This place hits all the right spots: service with a genuine smile, fabulously large portions of delicious south Indian cuisine, and an easy-on-your-wallet bill to top it all off. If you're not a fire-eater, beware of those brutal chillies and spices.

Palayok Restaurant
Opposite OCC

Filipino
24 797 290

It's a bit of a challenge to find Palayok, but once you do, you'll agree that the hunt was worth the effort. Fresh vegetables, fish and meat are perfectly seasoned and dressed in delicious sauces to create some of the finest Asian eating in Muscat.

Bar

Uptown
Opposite Golden Oryx

24 706 020

Dim lighting, sofa seating, the latest sporting events on a large TV screen, simple bar snacks and nightly entertainment and happy hour are all the ingredients you need for a good night out. Uptown is definitely worth a few drinks.

Al Bustan, Sidab & Qantab

Nestled in magnificent mountain settings, this is old-school Oman, and the ideal place to dine out.

Venue Finder

Arabic	Al Tanoor	p.166
Chinese	China Mood	p.168
Italian	Capri Court	p.168
Latin American	Samba	p.168
Moroccan	Shahrazad	p.169
Omani	Seblat Al Bustan	p.169
Seafood	Bait Al Bahr	p.167
Seafood	Beach Pavilion	p.167
Seafood	Blue Marlin	p.167
Bar	The Piano Lounge	p.169

Restaurants

Al Tanoor
Al Bandar Hotel

Arabic
24 776 666

It's worth the drive out of town just for the views from this beautiful restaurant, and the chance to see the stunning decor of the hotel itself. Offering an extensive Middle Eastern buffet, there is also a selection of Indian and vegetarian dishes, as well as live-cooking stations, where you can choose from fresh ingredients and watch as your meal is prepared.

Bait Al Bahr
Between Al Bandar & Al Waha Hotels

Seafood
24 776 666

If you fancy sampling some local delights from the sea surrounding you, Bait Al Bahr is a perfect choice. Bag a table on the veranda and cool off in the ocean breeze while you select from the mouth-watering menu. The emphasis is on succulent seafood, but there are some vegetarian choices too. Portions are on the small side, but decadently rich.

Beach Pavilion
Al Bustan Palace

Seafood
24 799 666

The Beach Pavilion's seashore location makes it a delightful place to enjoy a light lunch, watching the waves crash onto the shore as you tuck into good food. Home-baked rolls supplement smallish portions and the staff are only too happy to adjust a dish to suit your needs. Service is slow at weekends and holidays – in fact, it's so popular that you'll be lucky to get a table at all, so make sure you book in advance. Closed from June to September as it's simply too hot.

Blue Marlin
Marina Bandar Al Rowdha

Seafood
24 737 288

A haven of tranquillity, intimacy and serenity, this place takes advantage of its picturesque location. The modern European fare is fantastically prepared and presented, and is surpassed only by the service, which is top notch. The menu offers a good selection of seafood with a bit of a twist, as well some good non-fish dishes.

Capri Court
Al Bandar Hotel

Italian
24 776 666

Each table has its own breathing space at Capri Court, creating an elegant and relaxed atmosphere. The extensive menu and wine list are both aimed at the more discerning diner (and wallet). Portions are small but perfectly formed, and the pride taken in the presentation is obvious. Request a table outside and enjoy the sunset and the peaceful sound of the waves.

China Mood
Al Bustan Palace

Chinese
24 799 666

Acknowledged locally as one of the finest Chinese restaurants in Muscat, China Mood excels on many levels. For a start, the atmosphere is decadent and the staff are superbly attentive. The meat dishes are tender and juicy and the vegetables perfectly cooked and refreshingly free from the usual greasy oil slick. A fantastic place to enjoy a Far Eastern meal, although an early reservation is essential if you want to bag a table.

Samba
Al Waha Hotel

Latin American
24 776 666

South American cuisine is served up on a huge buffet with a selection of salads, seafood, grilled meats and vegetable dishes. An Asian corner doesn't quite fit in with the theme, but don't let that put you off tasting the oriental lamb, which is perfect. Try to save space for dessert – the chocolate fountain is worthy of a few repeat visits.

Seblat Al Bustan
Al Bustan Palace

Omani
24 799 666

At Seblat Al Bustan you can enjoy dinner in a Bedouin tent under the stars, between swaying palm trees on the hotel grounds. Traditional music and folk dancing, bread making, henna and handicrafts make this more of a cultural experience than just a meal. Be sure to try the shuwa, an Omani dish of slow-cooked meat, and finish the evening with traditional coffee and dates. Dinner is held every Wednesday night from September to May, from 19:30 to 23:00.

Shahrazad
Al Husn Hotel

Moroccan
24 776 666

From the shimmering walls of fabric dividing the tables to the splendid mosaic lanterns, this restaurant is the definitive in decadent dining. A simple but excellently prepared menu offers the pick of Moroccan cuisine and a wine list to match. Try the tajine for melt-in-the-mouth meat, with a side of fluffy couscous to soak up the delicately spiced juices. Delicious.

Bar

The Piano Lounge
Al Bandar Hotel

24 776 666

A very funky venue with white leather upholstery that is heaven to sink in to. Munch on feta cheese and olives as you peruse the generous cocktail menu or select a special creation. Laid-back tunes make this place great for a pre-dinner stop over or to simply show off your Jimmy Choos.

Madinat Sultan Qaboos

Expat haven and cultural delight, this spot has enough to tantalise.

Venue Finder

Arabic/Lebanese	Al Madina	p.170
Arabic/Lebanese	Kargeen Caffé	p.170
Chinese	Golden Dragon	p.170

Al Madina
MSQ Centre

Arabic/Lebanese
24 696 515

The buzzing place is fabulous at night when it's lit with candles and fairy lights. You can sit down on comfy majlis cushions inside, or enjoy the fresh air outside. Choose from sandwiches, mezze salads, pastries and fresh juices.

Golden Dragon
MSQ Centre

Chinese
24 697 374

Golden Dragon is an upmarket and attractive restaurant offering an extensive menu of Chinese and Thai dishes. Its specialities are highly recommended – try the range of starters served on a miniature wooden boat.

Kargeen Caffé
MSQ Centre

Arabic/Lebanese
24 692 269

This quaint, tented cafe is full of quirky ornaments and furniture, surrounded by greenery. The menu offers a variety of hearty soups, salads and Arabic appetisers, as well as burgers, and steaks for mains and a range of cakes and fruity drinks.

Clockwise from top left: Senior Pico's, Shiraz Restaurant, The Piano Lounge

Al Khuwayr

The fare is almost as impressive as the architecture in this part of town.

Venue Finder

Arabic/Lebanese	Fish Village	p.173
International	Alauddin Restaurant	p.172
International	Olivio's Coffee Shop	p.173
International	Tajin Grill	p.173
Omani	Bin Ateeq	p.172
Bar	Coral Bar	p.173

Restaurants

Alauddin Restaurant

International

Khalil Building · 24 600 667

This place is an absolute must-visit. Arrive with high expectations of a gastronomic good time. Excellent Indian, superb Arabic, mouth-watering Chinese and tasty continental cuisine is all served to deliciously high standards.

Bin Ateeq

Omani

Near Shell Petrol Station · 24 478 225

One of the friendliest and most welcoming restaurants in Muscat, Bin Ateeq serves Omani food at its best. The takeaway queue is testament to its popularity with the locals but dining in is worth the experience. It is messy, sticky-fingered stuff, so although you might not want to bring a first date here, it's well worth a visit on other occasions.

Fish Village
Opposite Radisson SAS

Arabic/Lebanese
24 480 918

This is a great little restaurant that is worth a visit for the view alone. The outside seating area is large, in a bustling area, with lots of locals congregating over shisha and a shawarma. Treat yourself to spicy squid, shish tawook or a sizzling tagine.

Olivio's Coffee Shop
Radisson SAS

International
24 707 207

This place offers more of an all-day-dining restaurant with simple, Mediterranean decor. Although there is an a la carte menu, you shouldn't miss out on one of the better buffets in town. This is the ideal location for a relaxed lunch.

Tajin Grill
Radisson SAS

International
24 707 207

Eating at Tajin is simple: just choose a succulent steak or some fresh fish or seafood, and then pick a sauce of your choice, a side order such as fries or a baked potato, and one of Tajin's flavoured butters.

Bar

Coral Bar
Radisson SAS

24 487 777

This piano bar has acts that change every few months, and fabulous underwater themed murals. The staff are very friendly, and the beers, spirits and wines are sold at standard hotel prices. A selection of salty nibbles will keep you thirsty.

Al Ghubbrah

The waterfront location and The Chedi's choice of restaurants make Al Ghubbrah a tasty destination.

Venue Finder

Cafe	Al Mas Brasserie	p.174
Cafe	The Lobby Lounge	p.175
International	Chedi Poolside Cabana	p.174
Mediterranean	The Restaurant	p.175

Al Mas Brasserie
Cafe
Bowshar Hotel   24 491 105

The sleek hotel decor sets the pace for this fabulous little cafe. Open most hours, this is more of a restaurant than quick coffee stop, and its menu is bursting with tempting Indian, Chinese and Arabic cuisine. Those wanting just a quick coffee can still nibble something from the small menu of snacks and light bites on offer.

Chedi Poolside Cabana
International
The Chedi Muscat   24 603 555

This is one of those places you're unlikely to find unless someone has told you to look for it – and it's worth looking for. The Cabana is a tranquil and intimate place to enjoy a cool evening breeze and a choice of set menus. The flavour is Mediterranean with a strong emphasis on seafood, served with finesse.

The Restaurant

The Lobby Lounge
The Chedi Muscat

Cafe
24 498 035

Situated just beyond the Majlis area at the entrance, the Lobby Lounge is an intimate arrangement of comfy seating areas in a brightly sunlit room. At night, the guests spill outside to bag one of the much envied tables around the giant gas fires in heavy black planters. A great place for an after dinner drink or sundowners.

The Restaurant
The Chedi Muscat

Mediterranean
24 524 400

The Restaurant boasts a fusion of contemporary Mediterranean, Arabic and Far Eastern decor, all aptly reflecting its menu. You can choose from sushi, tajin, fish or curries from one of the open kitchens, but leave room for the exquisite puddings and cakes. Prices are high, especially for alcohol, but the wine list is extensive.

Profile

178 Culture
182 History
186 Oman Today

Expect genuine warmth and smiles from the Omanis – theirs is a distinctive culture based on unrivalled hospitality.

People & Traditions

Oman has a unique culture influenced heavily by Islamic tradition as well as regional heritage. Its position on a historical trade route has meant the Omani population has been exposed to different cultures over the centuries. As a result, locals are tolerant, welcoming and friendly. Visitors are able to roam the souks and villages, the dress code is relatively liberal and women face little discrimination.

The official language is Arabic, but English is widely spoken, and most of the road signs and menus are bilingual.

Most Omanis wear traditional dress during work and social hours. Men wear an ankle length, collarless gown with long sleeves (dishdasha), usually in white. Traditional women's costumes are very colourful, and vary from region to region. In public, and more commonly, women wear normal clothes and cover this with a full-length, black cloak-dress (abaya). You can still see women wearing the 'burkha' (mask), which covers the brow, cheekbones and nose.

Religion

Islam is the official religion, with most following the Ibadhi sect, which is regarded as 'moderately conservative' and has the distinguishing feature of choosing a ruler by communal consensus and consent. In Oman, Sunni Muslims live primarily in Sur and the surrounding areas, as well as in Dhofar. There is also a Shi'a minority that live in the Muscat-Mutrah area.

Islam is a peaceful religion based on five basic principles (or pillars), including the main belief that there is only one God and that the Prophet Mohammed is his messenger.

The call to prayer is broadcast from the minarets of each mosque through loudspeakers, ensuring everyone knows it's time to pray. Friday is the holy day and you'll find that most of the country will slow down or stop until the early afternoon. Other religions are recognised and respected, and followers are free to practise their faith.

Ramadan

Ramadan is the holy month in which Muslims commemorate the revelation of the Holy Quran, the holy book of Islam. For 30 days Muslims are required to fast during daylight hours, abstaining from eating, drinking and smoking. In the evening, the fast is broken

Shisha

Smoking shisha (also known as water pipes, hookah pipes or hubbly bubbly, though formally known as nargile) is a popular and relaxing pastime in the Middle East and savoured in local cafes, while chatting with friends or to seal that delicious dinner. Shisha tobacco comes in a variety of aromatic flavours, such as strawberry, grape or the more popular apple.

with an Iftar, or feast. The start date of Ramadan is determined by the sighting of the moon and usually falls 11 days earlier than the previous year.

Non-Muslims are requested to respect this tradition and refrain from eating, drinking and smoking in public places, even in their cars, between sunrise and sunset, although most hotels will provide screened rooms for those not fasting. Be aware that bars are closed for the entire month and the sale of alcohol is prohibited.

Ramadan ends with a three-day celebration and holiday called Eid Al Fitr, or 'Feast of the Breaking of the Fast'.

Food & Drink

Traditional local cuisine is fairly simple, with rice as the main ingredient cooked together with beef, mutton, goat, chicken or fish, marinated in a blend of herbs and spices.

Arab cuisine is widely available as is western and Asian food, and the standard for meat eaters and vegetarians alike is generally high. Pork is forbidden in Islam; in supermarkets it is sold in a separate section, and restaurants must have special permission to serve it on their menus.

The consumption of alcohol is against Islamic law and it is forbidden for Muslims to drink or even handle it. However, the attitude to alcohol in Oman is far more relaxed than some other parts of the Middle East (such as the UAE emirate of Sharjah where it is prohibited completely) and you can buy alcoholic beverages in most hotels and some independent restaurants and clubs.

Clockwise from top right: Mosques in Kalbuh, Lamps in Mutrah

History

Situated on ancient trade routes and renowned for thoroughbred horses and frankincense, Oman has a history of prosperity and international influences.

The country's beginnings date back some 5,000 years, with archaeological evidence of an early form of civilisation. The name 'Oman' is said to come from the Arab tribes that first migrated to the area from a place in Yemen called Uman.

From the first to the third centuries, Oman was a prosperous seafaring nation. But tribal warfare over the election of a new Imam halted this expansion and Persian forces invaded the coastal areas.

The Portuguese arrived in 1507, with the aim of protecting supply lines to the east and to keep check of Omani trading power.

The country earned the title of the first and now oldest independent state in Arabia when Sultan bin Saif Al-Ya'arubi drove out the Portuguese first from Hormuz (1622) and then Muscat (1650).

From the 1600s to the 1800s, Oman vied with both Portugal and Britain for trade in the Gulf and Indian Ocean. During the Ya'arubi Dynasty (1624 to 1744), Oman entered an era of prosperity. Due to its excellent geographical position on some of the world's most lucrative and important trade routes, the country (particularly the southern part) became one of the wealthiest regions in the

Jabrin Fort

world. And then of course there was the trading in Arabian horses and the purest frankincense, both adding to an already flourishing economy.

The struggle for economic and political power continued until finally in 1744, Imam Ahmed bin Said (founder of the present Al Busaidi Dynasty) was elected by the collective of Omani tribes. He can credited with expelling the Persians, uniting the country, restoring Oman's fortune and making Muscat the country's capital.

The empire reached the height of its power in the mid 19th century under Sayyid Said bin Sultan. He extended control all the way to Zanzibar and Mombassa in Africa, and to parts of Persia, Pakistan and India.

Sayyid Said established political links with France, Britain and the US (the first Arab country to have ties with America). His death prompted the splitting of the empire between his two sons, one controlling Zanzibar (until its independence in 1861) and the other Muscat and Oman.

Sultan Qaboos came to power on July 23 1970, a day celebrated as Renaissance Day. Under his leadership, the Sultanate was able to end the Dhofar rebellion. Since then, the country has enjoyed peace and prosperity.

Development Of Islam

The Omanis were among the first Arabs to embrace Islam, back in 630AD, and the country became an Ibadhi state (following the Ibadhi sect of the Muslim religion) ruled by an elected religious leader, the Imam.

Oman Timeline

1508 Oman falls under Portuguese control

1659 The Ottoman Empire takes control of Oman

1744 Ottoman Turks are overthrown by Ahmed bin Said of Yemen, who becomes Imam and starts the leadership of the Al Busaidis, which remains to this day

1890 Oman becomes a British Protectorate

1962 Oil is discovered in Oman

1970 Sultan Qaboos comes to power as the Sultan of Oman

1971 Oman becomes a member of the United Nations and the Arab League

1981 Oman joins with other Gulf countries to form the Gulf Cooperation Council (GCC)

1984 Oman International Bank opens its doors

1986 Sultan Qaboos University opens

1996 Sultan Qaboos issues a decree clarifying the laws of royal succession and granting basic human rights to all citizens of Oman

1997 Two women are elected to the Consultative Council

1999 Oman and the UAE settle their border disputes

2000 Oman joins the World Trade Organisation (WTO)

2003 All Omani citizens over the age of 21 are given the vote

2004 The first female government minister is appointed

2006 Oman signs a free trade agreement with the USA

2007 Tropical Cyclone Gonu strikes Oman, causing widespread disruption

Oman Today

Oman is the essence of Arabia: stunning and unspoilt landscapes, rich marine life, a stable political climate and a culture honed by the desert sands.

A Ministry of Tourism was established in 2004, underscoring the sector's importance to the new economy. The slow growth in tourism is considered a good thing, since it has allowed more time to expand services and hotels to meet the demands of the modern traveller. The country is a successful model of how modernisation can be achieved without sacrificing local cultural identity. Oman's more than 500 forts, castles and towers are impressive tourist attractions, as are the international dune rallies, yacht races and annual festivals such as the Muscat Festival and the Khareef Festival in Salalah.

Fast-paced developments are a regional phenomenon, and Oman is no exception. Key projects include the upgrade of both Seeb and Salalah airports (www.omanairports.com), the new Six Senses Hideaway Zighy Bay (www.sixsenses.com), and Blue City, a new coastal city. The Wave (www.thewavemuscat.com) is set to become a new exclusive residential beachfront community near Muscat. This community will be part of an economic development including a marina, luxury hotels, a golf course, retail outlets and recreational areas.

For more information on Oman and what it has to offer, visit www.omantourism.gov.om.

Mutrah Corniche

Index

#

4WD	16

A

Abu Dhabi	110
Abu Dhabi Mall	138
Accommodation	32
Air	18
Airlines	18
Al-Araimi Complex	35, 138
Al-Munassir Naval Shipwreck	118
Al Ain	110
Al Alam Palace	61
Alauddin Restaurant	172
Al Bandar Hotel	34
Al Barouk	160
Al Busaidi Dynasty	184
Al Bustan	74, 166
Al Bustan Palace InterContinental Hotel	34
Al Deyar	160
Al Dhahirah Region	92
Al Dhalam Market	130, 142
Al Fair	85
Alfresco Restaurants	152
Al Ghazal Pub	163
Al Ghubbrah	174
Al Harthy Complex	138
Al Husn Hotel	34
Al Husn Souk	138
Al Jamal Health Club	124
Al Kawakeb Ayurveda Clinic	124
Al Kersa Fort	94
Al Khuwayr	80, 172
Al Madina	170
Al Madina Art Gallery	82
Al Maha Golf Course	122
Al Mas Brasserie	174
Al Nahda Resort & Spa	125
Al Nimer Tourism	108
Al Noorah Gardens	32
Al Qabil Rest House	32
Al Sawadi Beach Resort	35
Al Tanoor	166
Al Thowarah Hot Springs	94
Al Waha Hotel	35
Amouage Perfumery	86
Annual Events	29
Arabian Oryx Sanctuary	17
Arabian Sea Safaris	108, 119
Aramex	132
Art Galleries	46
As Seeb	86
ATMs	22
Automatic	155
Ayana Slim Spa	126

B

Bahla	95
Bahla fort	95
Bahwan Travel Agencies	108
Bait Al Bahr	167
Bait Al Zubair	56
Bait al Zubair Museum	10
Bait Muzna Gallery	56
Bait Naa'man	94
Bandar Al Jissah	76
Bander Khayran	118
Banks	22
Barka	94
Batinah Region	93
Beaches	47
Beach Hotel Apartments	32
Beach Pavilion	167
Beach Promenade	52
Bin Ateeq	172
Birthday of HM Sultan Qaboos	28
Blue City	186
Blue Marlin	167
Blu Zone Diving	119
Boat	19
Bollywood Chaat	155
Bowling Centre	115
Breakfast	152
Buffets	152
Bukha	99
Buraimi	92
Bus	19
Business	26

C

Café Glacier 154
Camel 8
Camel Racing 29
Capital Area Yacht 119
Capital Commercial Centre 55
Capital Store 134
Capri Court 168
Captial Commercial
  Centre (CCC) 138
Carpets 147
Car Rental 19
Car Rental Agencies 20
Caves 15
CBD 68
The Chedi Muscat 35
Chedi Poolside Cabana 174
Children's Museum 48
China Mood 168
China Town 156
Climate 22
Club Safari 163
Club Safari Rooftop Grill 156
Coastal Cruises 102
Cocktails 153
Copacabana 163
Copper Chimney 164
Coral Bar 173
Courier Services 25
Crime 22
Crowne Plaza Hotel Muscat 36
Crowne Plaza Resort Salalah 38
Culture 178
Currency Museum 68
Customs 26

D

D'Arcy's Kitchen 159
Dakhiliya Region 95
Daymaniyat Divers 119
Daymaniyat Islands 118
Desert Discovery Tours 108
DHL 132
Dhofar City Centre 136
Dhofar Park Inn International 32

Dhofar Region 96
Dhow Yard 14
Disabled Visitors 23
Diving 116
Dolphin & Whale Watching 102
Dolphins 6
Dos & Don'ts 24
Drinks 180
Drink Driving 24
Driving 20
Dubai 110
Duke's Bar 157
Dune Dinner Safari 104

E

East Coast 111
East Salalah 107
Eid Al Adha 28
Eid Al Fitr 28
Eihab Travels 108
Electricity 23
Empty Quarter Tours 108

F

Fahal Island 118
Fahal Island Swim 29
Fanja 130
Far Eastern Restaurant 160
Fish Village 173
Food 180
Foton World Fantasia 88
Full-Day Safari 104

G

Getting Around 18
Ghaba Rest House 32
Ghallah Wentworth Golf Club 122
Global Scuba 119
Golden Dragon 170
Golden Oryx 73, 164
Golden Oryx Tours 108
Golden Tulip Resort Khasab 38
Golden Tulip Seeb 36
Gold Souk 142
Golf 120

Grand Canyon of Oman Tours 108
Grand Hyatt Muscat 36
Green Mountain 165
Gulf Leisure 108, 119
Gulf Ventures Oman 108

H

Health Requirements 23
Heritage Sites 46
Hilton Salalah 39
Hisn Al Khandaq 93
History 182
Hormuzline Tours
  Company 108, 119
Horse Racing 29
Hotel Apartments 32

I

Ibadhi 178
Ibri 93
Ice Skating Centre 115
Imam Ahmed bin Said 184
Independent Restaurants 150
InterContinental Muscat 37
Internet 25
Islam 184

J

Jalali Fort & Mirani Fort 58
Jawaharat A'Shati 139

K

Kalbouh Park 62
Kargeen Caffé 170
kayak 116
Khareef Festival 30
Khasab 99
Khasab Travel & Tours 108, 119
Khayran 76
Khimji's Megastore 134
Khuwair Hotel Apartments 32

L

Landmark Group (City Plaza) 139
Le Mermaid Cafe 159

Live Music	153
Liwa Oasis	111
The Lobby Lounge	175
Local Cuisine	153
Lost City of Ubar	98

M

Madinat Sultan Qaboos	80, 170
Magazines	25
Magic Planet	88
Main Attractions	47
Majan Beach	52
Manam Hotel Apartments	32
Marah Land (Land of Joy)	50
Marco Polo Golf Course	122
Maria Theresa	70
Maria Theresa Thaler	70
Marina Café	155
Marjan Poolside Resteraunt	161
Markaz Al Bahja	139
Markets	142
Marks & Spencer	91
Mark Tours	108
Masirah Island	100
Money	24
Moon Light Diving Centre	119
Mosque Tours	104
Mountain Safari	105
Mughsail Beach	107
Mumtaz Mahal	55, 156
Musandam Cafe & Terrace	161
Musandam Extra Divers	119
Musandam Region	98
Muscat City Centre	140
Muscat Diving & Adventure Centre	108, 116
Muscat Diving & Adventure Centre	119
Muscat Festival	30
Muscat Gate Museum	58
Muscat Hills Golf & Country Club	120, 123
Muscat International Airport	18
Muscat Old Town	56
Museums	46

Mutrah	62
Mutrah Fish & Vegetable Market	144
Mutrah Fort	64
Mutrah Souk	144

N

Nakhal	94
Nasseem Park	88
National Museum	68
Natural History Museum	10, 80
Newspapers	25
Nizwa	12, 96, 107, 135
Nizwa Hotel	38
Nizwa Souk	145
Nomad Ocean	119

O

Olivio's Coffee Shop	173
Oman Air	18
Oman Dive Centre	17, 37, 119
Oman Heritage Gallery	147
Omani French Museum	58
Omani Museum	82
Omani Rial	24
Oman Society for Fine Arts	50
Oman National Championship	120
Oman National Transport Company	19
Oman Timeline	185
O Sole Mio	161
Ostrich Breeding Farm	94
Oudh	146
Overnight Desert Safari	106
Overnight Safari	105
Overnight Turtle Watching	105

P

Palayok Restaurant	165
Parks	47
Pavo Real	85
People	178
Perfume	146
The Piano Lounge	169

Post	25
Public Holidays	28

Q

Qantab	74, 166
Qara Mountains	98
Qurm	48, 154
Qurm Heights	154
Qurm Heights Park	52
Qurm Park & Nature Reserve	50

R

Radisson SAS Hotel	37
Rally Oman	30
Ramadan	179, 180
Ras Al Jinz Turtle Reserve	7
Religion	178
Rest Houses	32
The Restaurant	175
Restaurants for Kids	153
Riyam Park	64
Rub Al Khali	93
Rusayl	86
Rustaq	94
Rustaq & Batinah	108
Ruwi	68, 164
Ruwi High Street	73, 135

S

Sabco Commercial Centre	55, 140
Safaris	102
Safeer Hotel Suites	32
Safety	22
Salalah	16, 97, 136
Salalah Souk	136
Salman Stores	135
Samayil	130
Samba	168
Sayyid Said	184
Sea Taxis	76
Seblat Al Bustan	74, 169
Seeb Beach Park	88, 91
Seeb International Hotel	32
Senor Pico's	161
Shahrazad	169

Sharqiya Region 100
Shati Al Qurm 48, 158
Sheraton Oman Hotel 37
Shiraz 156
Shisha 179
Shopping Malls 138
Show Jumping 29
Sidab 74, 166
Silk Route 157
Silver 146
Sinbad's Wonder Centre 52
Sinbad the Sailor 13
Sirj Tea Lounge 159
Sir Ranulph Fiennes 98
Six Senses Hideaway
   Zighy Bay 186
Social Hours 26
Sohar 13, 95
Sohar Fort Museum 13
Souks 142
Souvenirs 147
The Spa 126
Spas 124
The Spa Bar For Men 126
Sports & Activities 114
Strait of Hormuz 99
The Sultan's Armed
   Forces Museum 70
Sultan bin Saif Al-Ya'arubi 182
Sultan Qaboos 184
Sultan Qaboos Grand Mosque 11
Sumail 96
Sur 14, 100
Suroor 130
Sur Plaza Hotel 39

T
Tajin Grill 173
Taxi 20
Telephone 25
Textiles 146
Time 26
Tipping 26
Tiwi 101
Tiwi Beach 101

Tomato 162
Tour Operators 108
Tours 102
Trader Vic's 162
Traditions 178
Treasure Tours Land &
   Sea Adventure 108
Tropicana 157
Turtle Beach Resort 17
Turtles 7
Tuscany 162

U
Ubar 98, 109
Uptown 165

V
Venue Directory 152
Visas 26

W
Wadi Drive 105
Wadis 9
Wadi Shab 101
Wadi Tiwi 101
Wahiba Desert 106
Wahibas Challenge 30
Walking 21
Water 23
Watersports 116
The Wave 186
Well-Being 124
West Salalah 107
Whales 6
Woodlands 165

Explorer Products

Residents' Guides

All you need to know about living, working and enjoying life in these exciting destinations

Coming in 2008/9: Bangkok, Brussels, Mexico City, Moscow, San Francisco, Saudi Arabia and Taipei

Mini Guides

Perfect pocket-sized
visitors' guides

Coming in 2008/9: Bangkok, Brussels, Mexico City, Moscow, San Francisco and Taipei

Activity Guides

Drive, trek, dive and swim... life will never be boring again

Check out www.explorerpublishing.com/products

Mini Maps

Fit the city in your pocket

Coming in 2008/9: Ajman, Al Ain, Bangkok,
Brussels, Fujairah, Mexico City, Moscow,
Ras Al Khaimah, San Francisco, Taipei,
Umm Al Quwain

Maps

Wherever you are, never get lost again

Photography Books
Beautiful cities caught through the lens

Lifestyle Products & Calendars
The perfect accessories for a buzzing lifestyle

Check out www.explorerpublishing.com/products

Explorer Team

Publishing
Publisher Alistair MacKenzie
Associate Publisher Claire England
Assistant to Associate Publisher Kathryn Calderon

Editorial
Group Editor Jane Roberts
Lead Editors David Quinn, Katie Drynan, Matt Farquharson, Sean Kearns, Tim Binks, Tom Jordan
Deputy Editors Helen Spearman, Jakob Marsico, Pamela Afram, Richard Greig, Tracy Fitzgerald
Senior Editorial Assistant Mimi Stankova
Editorial Assistants Grace Carnay, Ingrid Cupido

Design
Creative Director Pete Maloney
Art Director Ieyad Charaf
Design Manager Alex Jeffries
Senior Designer Iain Young
Junior Designer Jessy Perera
Layout Manager Jayde Fernandes
Designers Hashim Moideen, Rafi Pullat, Shawn Jackson Zuzarte
Cartography Manager Zainudheen Madathil
Cartographers Juby Jose, Noushad Madathil, Sunita Lakhiani
Traffic Manager Maricar Ong
Production Coordinator Joy Tubog

Photography
Photography Manager Pamela Grist
Photographer Victor Romero
Image Editor Henry Hilos

Sales & Marketing
Media Sales Area Managers Laura Zuffa, Stephen Jones
Corporate Sales Executive Ben Merrett
Marketing Manager Kate Fox
Marketing Executive Annabel Clough
Marketing Assistant Shedan Ebona
Digital Content Manager Derrick Pereira
International Retail Sales Manager Ivan Rodrigues
Retail Sales Coordinators Kiran Melwani, Sobia Gulzad
Retail Sales Supervisor Mathew Samuel
Retail Sales Merchandisers Johny Mathew, Shan Kumar
Sales & Marketing Coordinator Lennie Mangalino
Distribution Executives Ahmed Mainodin, Firos Khan
Warehouse Assistant Najumudeen K.I.
Drivers Mohammed Sameer, Shabsir Madathil

Finance & Administration
Finance Manager Michael Samuel
HR & Administration Manager Andrea Fust
Admin Manager Shyrell Tamayo
Junior Accountant Cherry Enriquez
Accounts Assistant Darwin Lovitos
Administrators Enrico Maullon, Kelly Tesoro
Drivers Rafi Jamal, Mannie Lugtu

IT
IT Administrator Ajay Krishnan
Senior Software Engineer Bahrudeen Abdul
Software Engineer Roshni Ahuja

Contact Us

▶ Reader Response
If you have any comments and suggestions, fill out
our online reader response form and you could win prizes.
Log on to **www.explorerpublishing.com**

▶ Newsletter
If you would like to receive the Explorer newsletter packed with
special offers, latest books updates and community news please
send an email to **Marketing@explorerpublishing.com**

▶ General Enquiries
We'd love to hear your thoughts and answer any questions
you have about this book or any other Explorer product.
Contact us at **Info@explorerpublishing.com**

▶ Careers
If you fancy yourself as an Explorer, send your CV (stating the
position you're interested in) to **Jobs@explorerpublishing.com**

▶ Designlab and Contract Publishing
For enquiries about Explorer's Contract Publishing arm and
design services contact **Designlab@explorerpublishing.com**

▶ Maps
For cartography enquries, including orders and comments,
contact **Maps@explorerpublishing.com**

▶ Corporate Sales
For bulk sales and customisation options, for this book or any
Explorer product, contact **Sales@explorerpublishing.com**

EXPLORER